EMOTIONRAISING

How to astonish, disturb, seduce
and convince the brain
to support good causes

Francesco Ambrogetti

civil sector press

Emotionraising: How to astonish, disturb, seduce and convince the brain to support good causes

First English Edition. Originally published in Italian by Maggioli S.p.A. 2013.

IMPORTANT:
The opinions expressed herein are solely those of the authors. To ensure the currency of the information presented, readers are strongly encouraged to solicit the assistance of appropriate professionals.

Further, any examples presented are intended only as illustrations. The authors, publishers and their agents assume no responsibility for errors or omissions or for damages arising from the use of published information or opinions.

ISBN 978-1-927375-38-9

Library and Archives Canada Cataloguing in Publication

Ambrogetti, Francesco, 1966-

[Emotionraising. English]
Emotionraising : how to astonish, disturb, seduce and convince the brain for good causes / Francesco Ambrogetti. — First English edition.
Translation of: Emotionraising: neuroscienze applicate al fundraising.
"Originally published in Italian by Maggioli S.p.A. 2013"—Title page verso.
Includes bibliographical references.
Issued in print and electronic formats.

ISBN 978-1-927375-38-9 (paperback).—ISBN 978-1-927375-39-6 (epub)

1. Fund raising. 2. Fund raising—Psychological aspects. I. Title. II. Title: Emotionraising. English.

HG177.A4313 2016 658.15'224 C2016-907082-4 C2016-907083-2

Emotionraising: How to astonish, disturb, seduce and convince the brain to support good causes

Published by Civil Sector Press Box 86, Station C, Toronto, Ontario, M6J 3M7 Canada
Telephone: 416.345.9403
www.charityinfo.ca

Publisher: Jim Hilborn
Edited by: Lisa MacDonald with Bonnie Munday
Book production: Cranberryink

Contents

PART ONE
The revolution in the brain: Emotions in marketing, decision-making and fundraising

PART TWO
Emotions at work: How to plan and implement campaigns and strategies that illuminate the mind, warm hearts—and open wallets

PART THREE
It's all over your face: How to recognize emotions during interaction with donors and supporters

PART FOUR
The good reasons and the real reasons: A conversation with Dan Hill on emotions and fundraising

FOREWORD

"The book you now hold
was written especially for you,
the scientist and artist of emotion."

Francesco Ambrogetti and his wonderful book *Emotionraising* have a special place in my affections, as well as on my bookshelf. He contributed almost a whole section for the special project I've recently assembled for the UK's Commission on the Donor Experience, on the theme of "the use and misuse of emotion." It's a subject close to the heart, for both of us.

That merely indicates that I think this book is very important, but it doesn't explain why.

The why is, because this book is about what works. And why it works when you do it properly.

I've been a professional fundraiser now for 40 years and a volunteer at it for a good few years before that. For much of this time I've been a consultant, renting myself and my colleagues out by the hour to any client disposed to pay the not unreasonable rates we asked for. This was so we could, as my long-term business partner George Smith would say, "sprinkle magic upon their fundraising." And we did just that, all over the world, in every continent except Antarctica.

There was one question that, at one time or another, every client without exception would ask. Always we'd have been steering them towards one or maybe several new or improved ways to fundraise, or new strategies to apply to old ways. And the clients, always, would say, "Yes. OK. That sounds fine. But will it work, for us?"

I would invariably answer in the same way, always. "Yes," I would reply, "for sure it will work. But only if you do it properly."

The client would then go away and come back weeks, months, or even years later and say, "You told me that 'such-and-such' would work, and it didn't."

"Ah," I would respond, "that's not quite precise. I didn't just say it would work. I said it would work *if you do it properly*."

Then as often as not the client then would look at me a little bashfully, mumble something incomplete or incoherent, then leave.

Hopefully they'd learned a lesson. Fundraising will only ever work if you do it properly.

It's not rocket science. Really it isn't. It's more about making someone feel, for real. It is about astonishing, persuading, seducing and even disturbing. As American fundraiser Jeff Brooks puts it, getting people to give to a cause is not about, "Careful, clean, precise forms of writing. Fundraising belongs to a much messier, more passionate world that includes love letters, ransom notes, pleas for mercy and outbreaks of religious fervour."

Emotionraising will help you to gain entry to that much more interesting world.

But there is some science to it and that science is fascinating, as Francesco Ambrogetti shows. As you'll learn, you need to grasp at least the essence of this science if you are to excel at emotional fundraising.

Mostly the subject of this book, raising money effectively by understanding and taking account of emotions, is all about *what works*.

That's what a firm grasp of emotional fundraising will give you – an understanding of what will work in your fundraising communications and why. And what won't work and why not.

So the content of what you are now holding could be literally priceless. In the right hands, of course.

In this book the author says, "This book is for fundraisers, but also for all who work to make this world a little better because they could understand that emotions are not something to hide, to control, or to be ashamed of, but rather constitute the 'salt' of what we do."

This leads neatly back to the quote that I put at the top of this foreword.

Fundraisers are indeed scientists and artists of emotions. If we understand that and manage those emotions right we will make people happy and make ourselves happy at the same time. And for all our sakes we'll enable the great causes that we work for to make more of a difference, so that faster and more surely they can change the world for the better.

And that has to be really, really worth doing.

This book will work its magic for you, too, but not if you keep it neatly stacked on your bookshelf or tucked away in your bottom drawer. So get it out there, into hands, bags and briefcases and onto bedside tables. Lend your copy widely, or better still, buy one each for all your colleagues. Expect to see it passed around the office bristling with post-it notes. Get it extra-well thumbed and opened by asking each colleague at suitable intervals, "how has *Emotionraising* changed how you view and do your job?"

You'll learn a lot from the answers.

I commend this book to you, in all its wonderfulness.

Ken Burnett
London N5
October 2016

INTRODUCTION

What do I ask of a painting?
I ask it to astonish, disturb,
seduce, convince.

—Lucian Freud

1.

This book originates from my curiosity and professional practice to convince other people, often total strangers to me, to give me some of their most precious and intimate things—including money—to support a cause, an idea or an organization. My job is, in fact, to explain, excite, seduce and convince someone around a cause or a social project and convince him or her to open their wallets, to give me their credit card and even persuade their friends or family to do the same. Having worked with so many different organizations—AIDS, children, indigenous peoples, and animals—I often wondered why sometimes it is easier to get a yes to an appeal for funds, or why certain campaigns have more success than others. How is it that certain causes or organizations are more popular than others in terms of money raised or social media views? Is it just that some are better at utilizing sales techniques, a bit like circus magicians or door-to-door sales representatives?

The fact is that, practically every day, we give money to a charity, or support someone, sign up for something, or advise others to adopt a cause, a baby, a kitten or an organization. It depends on the data and their reliability,[1] but it is estimated that in the world in 2015:

- 2.4 billion people helped a stranger in difficulty;
- 1.5 billion people made at least one financial donation;
- 1.1 billion people volunteered

In short, instead of so many odious taxes, why don't governments launch a good fundraising campaign? Why do people give and continue to donate?

Usually when we do not have convincing answers to behaviour and social

---

1. https://www.cafonline.org/docs/default-source/about-us-publications/1950a_wgi_2016_report_web_v2_241016.pdf?sfvrsn=4

phenomena we turn to opinion polls. How many people believe in God? Which candidate will you vote for in the next election? How many people trust or agree with this statement or with that proposal? The same applies to generosity or charitable donations. If we want to understand why people give, and to which causes or organizations, usually we look at the latest polls.

Assuming that the results are statistically correct and representative of the population, they leave us with more questions than answers. Among the reasons to donate (I have come to count more than 40!), the most frequent are the following:

- I want to help people in trouble.
- I want to support a cause I believe in.
- I want to help to solve a problem that affects me personally (or affects a family member or friend).
- It is part of my education or tradition (such as a religion).
- I have been asked by someone I trust (friend or family, etc.).

The fact is that these are just opinions, i.e., rational responses or reflections in retrospect after we made the donation, and do not reveal anything about what exactly and intimately has pushed us to act so strangely, like giving $10 to a stranger or giving our credit card details without buying any product or service, without having anything in return.

In general, many market researchers and business leaders today tend not to trust most of the polls. And given the mistakes of many exit polls in accurately predicting election results, they have good reason! Studies have shown that 50 percent to 70 percent of those who respond to online surveys provide incomplete answers, while other research has found that 75 percent of participants in focus group tend to go against their own perceptions and opinions and adapt to what other people think.[2]

The question therefore is: If we cannot ask through an interview or a questionnaire why we support a cause or give money, how can we understand what moves us to do so?

For centuries, philosophers, economists, theologians, psychologists and ordinary people have wondered and constructed theories to explain the abnormal behaviour of sharing something valuable (like our money and our time) with strangers, without receiving anything in return. Several researchers and scientists have spent their time and careers trying to better understand the paradox created by those individuals who do something for free and voluntarily for a common good—for example, cleaning a beach or a public garden or helping someone to

---

2. Dan Hill, *Emotionomics: Leveraging emotions for business success*, Revised edition, Kogan Page, 2008.

cross the street. From the perspective of the Cartesian theory of rationality (Cogito ergo sum), the *homo economicus* of John Stuart Mill and Ricardo, and also from the evolutionary point of view of Darwinian survival of the fittest, the fact that someone gives something to a stranger without an equivalent in return has posed serious problems, to the point that some of these scholars had to develop specific theories explaining this "paradox." The theory of the "free rider" developed by economist Mancur Olson identifies precisely this paradox of collective action. In a nutshell, if individuals are natural "free riders" because they can benefit from a public good that others will generate (a park, a school, etc.), why do people still collectively act, through a donation for example, to support causes, programs and initiatives knowing that others will pay for it?[3]

To some economists, however, giving is simply a selfish act: donate for cancer research because I have the chance of being impacted in the future and therefore I could benefit from research advancement. But why do we give to individuals, communities, animals, museums, etc., with whom we have no connection, nor ever will have the chance to see them or know them? Other economists and psychologists, such as James Andreoni,[4] maintain that the act of giving to unknown entities and individuals is not totally free; rather it is an act motivated by increasing self-esteem. The act of giving allows us to be perceived as a better person (or considered by others to be better because we're generous), and therefore giving is a bit like being pampered—like putting on a nice pair of gloves to warm our cold hands (the "warm glow theory").

2.

But if giving is not a rational choice and is not a self-esteem mechanism, because many people give anonymously – let's think about $1 billion donated for victims of disasters in remote parts of the world, or for a rare disease such as ALS through the Ice Bucket Challenge—why do we keep giving money?

It is interesting to note in fact that donations grown or remained stable even during periods of economic crisis such as the recent ones. While philosophers, economists and theologians formulated their ideas to explain the "anomaly" of giving, neurosciences with their capacity to look into what is really happening in the brain while we do things like giving money have changed everything. Understanding what really happens in our brains changed everything, not only

---

3. Mancur Olson, *The Logic of Collective Action: Public Goods and the Theory of Groups*, Harvard University Press, 1st ed., 1965; 2nd ed. 1971.
4. Andreoni, James (1990): "Impure Altruism and Donations to Public Goods: A Theory of Warm-Glow Giving," *Economic Journal* 100 (401): pages 464–477. JSTOR 2234133.

from an evolutionary or cognitive perspective, but especially from the philo-
sophical and moral point of view that is behind philanthropic behaviour. Antonio
Damasio,[5] a Portuguese neurologist, had the audacity based on neuroscience to
refute in a wonderful book the foundation itself of modern Western identity. The
cogito ergo sum of Descartes, Damasio argues, is a big mistake and a deception. In
fact, our decisions are taken not by the "cogito" or rational part of the brain, but
from that part of the brain that deals with emotions, which in turn is activated by
the body on the basis of sensory input (sight, hearing, taste, smell, touch).

In short, we decide on instinct or in a "blink," as Malcom Gladwell would say,
and only after the rational part of the brain formalizes and explains our decision
through words and concepts. This finding, subsequently confirmed in recent years
by many studies and experiments, has radically changed the way we communicate
and do marketing and also how to do fundraising. Because now we really know
that emotions, whose etymological origin from Latin *movere* means "take action,
moving toward something or someone" physically, are the ones that decide if
you will press the button "Donate" or "like" on Facebook; if you'll dial a phone
number in order to "adopt" a child; if you send a text message; or if you will open
your portfolio to a young stranger at the subway exit.

3.

A note on the subject of the emotions is that this is a universal human trait
that is hard-wired in our body and brain and it's trans-cultural. Emotions are
programmed into our DNA to lead our behaviour and actions, and are not an
exclusive element of Italian folklore or Mediterranean culture.

It is true however, that as an Italian who has lived abroad for so long and
comes from a family with its remote origins in Sicily, emotions for me are an
obvious fact of life. I grew up and I was fed by stories, music, images and highly
emotional food. I still remember the days spent in the kitchen surrounded by
dozens of women who told incredible stories of Noto, a small Sicilian village and
jewel of European Baroque, moving from laughs to tears in seconds—all in strict
Sicilian dialect and songs.

When I speak or write about emotions, the reaction of non-Italians is often
as follows: "Obviously you talk about emotions because you are Italian: look how
you gesticulate, listen to your tone of voice, think about the drama of the opera
or of a football match. We (Germans, Anglo-Saxon, Nordic, Asians, etc.) have
different behaviours and express ourselves differently. We are more 'cold' and

---

5. Antonio Damasio, *Descartes' Error: Emotion, Reason, and the Human Brain*, Putnam, 1994.

reserved." The truth is that, as neuroscience and marketing shows, emotions are a universal evolutionary trait that are not at all determined by culture. Of course, how to cry, laugh or get angry changes depending on the geographical context, culture and language, but all human beings feel biologically the same emotions and react in the same ways. In fact, we can read the emotions on faces of people no matter where they come from, their educational level or their social background, and we can recognize the same emotions on their faces even if they are blind.

I have met over the years thousands of large and small donors from Germany, Sweden, England, Argentina, Thailand, Australia, etc., and I've seen how some stories, causes or specific campaigns provoke equally anger, disgust, surprise or joy. These emotions then leads them to do something like donate or support a cause or an organization, at any latitude, culture or climate. An interesting anecdote is what happened to me during the International Fundraising Congress (IFC), which is held in the Netherlands every year and is the world's leading conference for the fundraiser. Before starting the session on emotions, a tall blond gentleman wearing a business suit approached me very formally and told me: "I am the president of a German organization, and we think this type of thing does not work in our country." Without arguing, I thanked him for coming and invited him to attend the workshop. During the session, while I was showing examples of very emotional campaigns and videos, I heard sobs coming from the room and when I turned around I saw the same German man with red eyes trying to conceal his tears. He looked at me, smiled and gave me the OK sign saying, "You were right. Even Germans get emotional."

4.

This book is based on the recent discoveries in neuroscience applied to marketing and fundraising that show how our brain—both when we buy a product, and when we make a donation or subscribe to a petition—decides on the basis of some specific emotions activated in that part of the brain called the meso-limbic system (the one that controls our heartbeat, oversees memories and reacts to stimuli and rewards such as food, sex, or money). Using more than 20 years of my experience in Italy and around the world, in which I've raised millions of dollars, pesos, yen and euros for large and small social causes, we will try together to figure out why and how emotions guide our decisions and what role they play when we decide to support or join certain causes or organizations. We will do this using practical and real examples of success (but also resounding flops and mistakes). We will explain how the ability to thrill, surprise and excite somebody is the key to everything we do and in particular is the decisive element activated when we do something to help others.

5.

In the first part of the book, we will discover how neuroscience have revolutionized the assumptions about why we act and why we give, and we'll see how modern marketing and fundraising theories and tactics are increasingly using content and emotional strategies. We will discover the six key emotions that are activated when someone decides to make a donation. In the second part, through examples of successful fundraising campaigns online and offline, we will better understand how to practice emotions in fundraising and how emotions are activated through the use of images, sounds, smells and specific words. In the third part, inspired by Dan Hill's book "Emotionomics" and the television series "Lie to Me," we will see how emotions can be "revealed" or understood through the study of micro-facial expressions and body language. Finally, we will have the opportunity to have a chat with some of the world's leading experts on emotions applied to marketing and fundraising.

6.

Between the publication of the first edition of this book in Italy (2013) and this edition, a lot has happened. I worked in Asia where I saw the power of emotions in one part of the world, which seems to us so far away from emotions. I returned to Italy, the land of emotions, and in the past three years I had the opportunity to discuss with neuroscientists and hundreds of fundraisers the subjects of the book in international congresses and during a chat over a glass of wine. I have experienced even more deeply the use of emotions applied to fundraising campaigns, and for the first time I have seen and measured what happens in the brain of a potential donor when he is making a legacy to a charity. All this has greatly enriched the contents of this book, which has been expanded and improved. But surely "Emotionraising" has not changed in its core substance and main assumptions, and each time I present, not only do I manage to get the public emotional, but I meet many people who say, "Why haven't I thought of that?"

7.

This book is for fundraisers, and for anyone working to make this world a little better because they understand that emotions are not something to hide, control or be ashamed of, but rather they constitute the "salt" of what we do. After all, we are all, a little bit, scientists and artists of emotions in order to astonish, disturb, seduce and persuade others to do something that will make someone happy—and make us happy at the same time.

PART ONE

The revolution in the brain: Emotions in marketing, decision-making and fundraising

"I would like my children to be able
to understand the emotions of others,
their insecurities, their anguish,
their hopes and their dreams."

- Lady Di

CHAPTER 1

From Darwin to Gladwell: How neuroscience has revolutionized the way we communicate with consumers, donors and companies

When was the last time you had a discussion with a management board, with your boss or colleagues from communication or brand because they believed that the images for the last campaign were "too strong"? And do you remember when you tried to control your rapid heartbeat and sweating in front of a crowd or a donor when you told the story of someone that they would like to help? And you've probably been ashamed when you felt the tears in your eyes seeing images such as children who have tragically died or puppies that have been neglected.

I was somewhat perplexed asking myself these questions when, some years ago, the case of Karen Klein of New York state had exploded. The video showed Karen, a nice woman whose job is to control acts of vandalism on public transport, being the victim of a bullying episode by a group of teenagers. The video went viral and caused such a reaction (more than 2 million have seen it on YouTube) $750,000 was raised in just few weeks, above the original target of $5,000 that had been established by the organizers to give a nice trip to Karen. In comparison, multimedia campaigns for known organizations (such as those starring Angelina Jolie as testimonials for UNHCR in the case of the flood in Pakistan) have attracted far fewer people and collected less money.

I discussed this phenomenon with some colleagues, and some of them were really angry. "You know," they said, "we stress ourselves out to raise money for emergencies and humanitarian disasters, or to find a cure for a disease that kills millions of innocent people, and this lady is able to raise millions of dollars to take a vacation?" The truth is that this campaign was not orchestrated by a guru of social media, was not meant to be a prize winner by a creative advertising agency nor had it been designed, alas, by a professional fundraiser. And yet it had the power to generate emotion—anger—that mobilized millions of people who wanted to try to do something to find a remedy for the woman insulted and mistreated, including through making a donation. It must be said that Karen and the organizers of this campaign have created a foundation that fights bullying, and have not spent that money on a vacation.

The examples are endless: Think of the waves of emotion that shook the world on Boxing Day 2004 during the tsunami in South East Asia; or, more recently, the Ice Bucket Challenge for ALS; and even the fund in memory of the UK member of parliament Jo Cox, who was brutally murdered on the eve of the EU referendum, which collected more than 1.5 million pounds in a few days. In all these cases, supported by real-time dissemination on TV and social media, the emotional wave mobilized so many people in generating an immediate reaction. (Remember, the origin of the word emotion means generating a share, a movement: when you get emotional, you cannot stand still contemplating; you are forced to act and react).

In all these cases, the reaction was to do something to help, to alleviate suffering, to share the pain. And one of the tools at our disposal to do so is to donate with a text message, an email, a phone call or a bank deposit. Yet if we look at the hard data, the number of people affected by events such as those mentioned is far lower than the number who are affected by diseases such as AIDS, tuberculosis and malaria, for which the funds raised are often much less.

EVENT	YEAR	FUNDS RAISED IN $
LIVE AID (TV UK and US)	July 1985	250 million
09/11 (US)	September 2001	1.4 billion
Tsunami (Asia Pacific)	December 2004	2.9 billion
Hurricane Katrina	April 2009	4 billion
Haiti earthquake	January 2010	1.2 billion
Ice Bucket Challenge	August 2014	115 million

Fig. 1.1. Events, Campaigns and Fundraising.

Major emergencies have moved the generosity of many in recent years (also thanks to media coverage). However, thanks to social media, now also relatively new and unknown organizations such as the campaign by Invisible Children's KONY or charity:water are successful in no time, without famous testimonials or great media exposure, but thanks in great part to strong emotional content.

Neuroscience finally discovered that emotions, rather than being something to hide or to be controlled, guide our decisions. In this chapter we will summarize the main discoveries of neuroscience and how they have been applied to communication, marketing and fundraising, but also more in general how they apply to our lives. Well-known scientists such as Malcolm Gladwell or Daniel Goleman, and the Nobel prize winner Daniel Kahneman, based most of their success on the study and dissemination of how emotions work—just like Walt Disney, Steven Spielberg, Lucian Freud, Roberto Benigni and Barack Obama, to name some of the contemporary masters of emotions. There is no better animated film than "Inside Out" that translates the complexity of emotions into a successful movie for kids and adults.

From the heart to the brain: How the neuroscience revolution has changed the understanding of human behaviour

The revolution brought by the neurosciences in the last 20 years was of such importance that the main pioneers are still trying to understand how wide the potential impact is and its applications. Obviously, a lot of this untapped potential opens up fascinating scenarios and practical applications for the treatment of autism or schizophrenia. But the discovery of bio-chemical functioning of the brain and nervous systems (through tools such as MRI) has revolutionary applications on how to communicate with the public and influence behaviour. In an attempt to outline the history of this revolution as it applies to marketing and fundraising, we can summarize, using Dan Hill reconstruction,[6] the main steps in the following table. It shows the parallel path of the discoveries of neuroscience and its application to psychology, economics and marketing.

Neuroscience

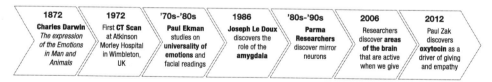

1872	1972	'70s-'80s	1986	'80s-'90s	2006	2012
Charles Darwin *The expression of the Emotions in Man and Animals*	First **CT Scan** at Atkinson Morley Hospital in Wimbleton, UK	**Paul Ekman** studies on **universality of emotions** and facial readings	**Joseph Le Doux** discovers the role of the **amygdala**	**Parma Researchers** discover mirror neurons	Researchers discover **areas of the brain** that are active when we give	Paul Zak discovers **oxytocin** as a driver of giving and empathy

Marketing, TV and Advertising

1998	2002	2005	2007	2008	2009	2015
Daniel Goleman *Emotional Intelligence*	**Daniel Kahneman** Nobel Prize for economics for the role of emotions	**Malcolm Gladwell** *Blink* on the role of emotions in decision making	**Dan Hill** *Emotionomics* on the role of emotions in marketing	UK Institute of Advertising successful marketing is emotional	Fox TV series "Lie to Me"	Disney cartoon "Inside Out"

Fig. 1.2. The Discovery of Emotions.

---

6. Hill, Dan. *Emotionomics, Leveraging Emotions for Business Success*. Revised edition, Kogan Page, 2008. Dan Hill, *About Face: The Secrets of Emotionally Effective Advertising*. Kogan Page, 2010.

It's interesting to note that Charles Darwin and Adam Smith, who perhaps are commonly identified as the pioneers of selfishness theories, have in fact been inspiring pioneers in the study of emotions.

The father of the theory of evolution, Darwin, was surprised when noting the similarity between the expressions on his child's face and that of monkeys.[7] Darwin spent many years observing patients in various psychiatric hospitals, comparing their expressions with those of animals. In his book, The *Expression of the Emotions in Man and Animals*, Darwin believes and is able to prove scientifically that animals feel emotions. Emotions are programmed or hardwired into the DNA of the biological species and are not a cultural thing: they activate neural circuits, and trigger similar behavioural reactions and physical and physiological changes experienced by both animals and men.

But the most important part of Darwin's work is when he showed that emotions—as they are expressed or can be identified through our facial expressions—are universal, and are not determined by culture or geographical context. It will also be demonstrated in subsequent studies (by Ekman and others) that the emotions are the same even in populations that have never had or known written language and, as some researchers have recently discovered in California, emotions are the same even among people who are blind.[8] Emotions are not learned like the language, writing, or other rational forms.

However, it was not until almost a century later, in the 1960s, when Paul Ekman[9] and Wally Friesen of the University of San Francisco were able to classify all of the underlying facial expressions of emotions.

The two scientists have developed the Facial Action Coding System (FACS), which codifies the movements of the 43 facial muscles that create 23 units of action that move our facial muscles when we feel certain emotions. The Ekman system, on which the successful television series "Lie to Me" was based, has systematized emotions—expressed through the micro expressions of the face—that take place in the unconscious part of the brain. Ekman made the first connection between the decisions and actions we take every day on one side of the brain and the emotional part that's activated on the other.

Our true feelings trigger our behaviour and our very first decisions before we

---

7. Darwin, Charles. (1998), *The Expression of the Emotions in Man and Animals*, third edition, London: Harper Collins.
8. Willingham, Bob and David Matsumoto. "Spontaneous Facial Expressions of Emotion of Congenitally and Noncongenitally Blind Individuals," *Journal of Personality and Social Psychology*, 2009. Vol. 96, No. 1, 1–10.
9. Ekman, Paul. *Emotions Revealed: Recognizing Faces and Feelings to Improve Communication and Emotional Life*, Second Edition, Holt Paperbacks; 2nd edition 2007.

realize it. We then rationalize and give an explanation and a name to how and why we acted in a certain way. Later, we'll explore extensively the subject of micro-facial expressions, because knowing or being able to read emotions through facial expressions is a formidable tool for understanding whether our messages and our efforts to convince someone to buy a product or to donate are working.

In June 2014, Paul Ekman sent a survey to 248 of the most active emotion researchers in the world to establish a consensus on universality of emotions.

Of those who responded, 90 percent agreed that there are universal emotions—emotions that all humans, no matter where we live or how we were raised, have in common.

- **91% said anger is universal**
- **90% said fear is universal**
- **86% said disgust is universal**
- **80% said sadness is universal**
- **76% said enjoyment is universal**

The most interesting development of Ekman's research is the project Atlas of Emotions,[10] a project started with the Dalai Lama. As Ekman said, "It was created to increase understanding of how emotions influence our lives, giving us choice (at least some of the time) about which emotion we are experiencing, and how our emotions influence what we say and do. While emotions are central to our lives—providing the joy, alerting us to threats, a force for change, a warning against what is toxic, and calling to others for help—we do not choose what to feel or when to feel it. The Atlas of Emotions was created to give us awareness of our emotions, and sometimes even some choice about what we are feeling, through better understanding of how emotions work."

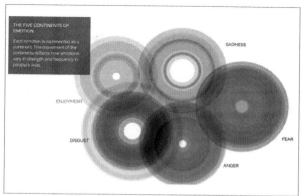

Fig. 1.3. "Atlas of Emotions" according to Ekman.

10. http://www.paulekman.com/atlas-of-emotions/

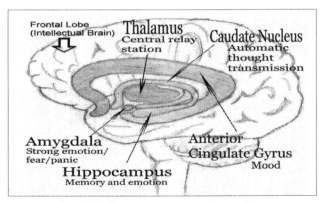

Fig. 1.4. Brain components governing emotions.

More interesting is the definition of emotions by Ekman: "An episode of emotion is a brief, succinct experience, one which does not always fit our expectations. Most emotions arise in under a twenty-fifth of a second and last no longer than a few minutes. Often we feel as though our emotions last much longer; however, what we are remembering is likely a series of emotion episodes." This is why in fundraising it's so crucial to transform emotions into feelings so to lead and repeat the same actions.

The definition of emotion for Ekman? It's "A process, in particular a kind of very fast, automatic appraisal influenced by our evolutionary and personal pasts, in which we sense that something important to our welfare is occurring and a set of physiological changes and behaviours begin to deal with the situation. In particular, different emotions efficiently coordinate response systems, thereby helping us respond to important challenges or opportunities."

Just as Darwin did not invent "social Darwinism," Adam Smith, one of the fathers of the modern economy with his "invisible hand" and theory that the individual only pursues his own interest, was thoroughly focused on emotions.[11] Smith was intrigued by empathy, this extraordinary capacity of human beings to experience the same pain and the same emotions of other human beings with similar experiences. In other words, maybe Smith had identified the first "mirror neurons," which will be discussed extensively later. And his preliminary research inspired many neuroscience and behavioural economics studies and theories.

As Nicolas Baumard, a Research Scholar in the Department of Cognitive

---

11. http://www.cognitionandculture.net/home/blog/16-nicolas/760-adam-smith-1723-1790-on-mirror-neurons-and-empathy.

Sciences at the École Normale Supérieure in Paris, put it: "Smith thought that our capacity to experience feelings about the feelings of others was the basis of social life. In fact, his Theory of Moral Sentiments starts with these words, 'How selfish so ever man may be supposed, there are evidently some principles in His nature, which interest him in the fortune of others, and render their happiness necessary to him, though he derives nothing from it except the pleasure of seeing it. Of this kind is pity or compassion, the emotion which we feel for the misery of others, when we either see it, or are made to conceive it in a very lively manner. That often we derive sorrow from the sorrow of others, is a matter of fact too obvious to require any instances to test it.'"

In modern times, no one has succeeded more than Malcolm Gladwell in popularizing how emotions play an essential role in our lives. His book *Blink*[12] was a success and a milestone in explaining how emotions and decisions in life are closely related. Using recent discoveries of neuroscience and dozens of anecdotes and stories from real life, Gladwell explains how we decide in two to three seconds—in a blink, in fact—and then we rationalize and explain rationally why or what we did. According to Gladwell we decide by selecting a tiny amount of information, mostly visual. These decisions are guided by the right side of the brain, the unconscious, which has to do with emotions. One of the stories Gladwell mentions in his book is that of art expert Federico Zeri, who recognized immediately, at first sight, without examining them, the false kouros purchased by the Getty Museum. The decision of Zeri was not based on any specific analysis, and he did not analyze specific findings on the statues, but he then revealed it as a correct judgment call, explained by his "gut feeling"—the emotional (physical) side that guides our decisions well before they reach the rational part of the brain.

We will learn how to better understand the implications of the most recent discoveries of neuroscience on what happens in our brains when we decide to donate. But to do that, we will first make a brief digression to summarize which parts of the brain are the parts that govern our emotions, our decisions and our intention to be altruistic or to donate to various causes and organizations.

---

12. Gladwell, Malcom. *Blink: The Power of Thinking without Thinking*, Back Bay Books, Little, Brown, January 11, 2005

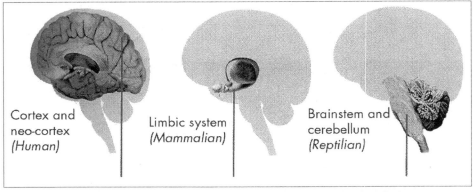

	Neocortex	Limbic System	Original Brain
Processing Mode	Reflective	Behavioral	Gut Reaction
Processing Level	Conscious	Subconscious	Subconscious
Function	Gives Meaning	Assigns Value	Matches Patterns
Contextual Basis	Cultural Norms	Past Experience	Universal
End Result	Provides Reason	Adjusts Actions	Fight or Flight

Fig. 1.5. The 3 brains and the emotional brain, according to Dan Hill.

First, emotions are located in the most primitive part of the brain, the limbic system, that operates by influencing both the endocrine system and the nervous system.[13] This system—in particular, the amygdala and the hippocampus—through training and memory recall, operates and activates many of the so-called primordial decisions (such as escape when we face danger or fight to defend ourselves, cry, laugh, etc.). The same system stimulates the release of the "drugs" or chemicals in the blood that are involved in reward and punishment (e.g., dopamine, epinephrine).

The limbic system is closely connected to the prefrontal cortex (which presides over movements and decisions) and therefore there is a close connection between the decision based on emotional reactions and actual physical movement (emotions as a word has the same root of movement). While the hippocampus "remembers" facts, recalling similar experiences, the amygdala will judge the emotional value. The amygdala then provides each sensory stimulus (sight in the first place, but also smells, sounds, touch, etc.) with the right level of attention, enriches it with emotions and, finally, stores it in the form of memory. The

---

13. Le Doux, Joseph. *The Emotional Brain (The Mysterious Underpinnings of Emotional Life)*, Simon & Schuster, Touchstone 1998

hippocampus, then, through the amygdala stimulation, activates the nervous system (heart rate, breathing, salivation, tears, etc.). And then the motor system (action) is active well before the cortex (the part of brain formed more recently and presiding over language, calculation, etc.) is activated.

Latest news from the brain labs: How emotions govern our actions and our empathy

The neurosciences are an endless source of discoveries about how our minds works. Among other things, scientists have discovered the mechanisms that trigger seemingly irrational behaviour such as compassion for others or giving money for nothing in return. Over the past 20 years, numerous studies have helped to map what part of the brain is involved when we do certain things, including when we decide to donate to some causes or an organizations.

Among the pioneers who have applied or contributed to applying the discoveries of neuroscience to generosity and identifying mechanisms that govern the decision to donate, we can cite at least three scientists, or rather three groups of scientists.

1. The first is a group of Italian researchers from the University of Parma, led by Professor Giacomo Rizzolatti, who discovered in the 1990s the so-called "mirror neurons." Those "neurons" light up when we see others suffering, laughing, etc., even when we observe them in virtual form—for example, in a photograph or on a TV screen, or in our imagination when we listen to a story.

2. The second scientist is Paul Zak, a neuroscientist and economist at Claremont University in California who discovered the functioning of the so-called "love molecule," or oxytocin. This is a hormone that increases our capacity for empathy toward others and increases in our blood when, for example, we are making a donation or engaged in an act of generosity toward others.

3. The third is a group of neuroscientists from the universities of Bethesda in Maryland, Genoa and Rio de Janeiro. They have shown what part of the brain (mesolimbic system) is activated when we give money. There is a release of positive and chemical stimuli equal to what happens when we receive a monetary reward, eat a good meal or engage in sexual intercourse.

Mirror neurons: Do you feel what I'm feeling? A group of Italian researchers from the University of Parma (Rizzolatti and others)[14] discovered mirror neurons. They are so important that a famous neuroscientist Vilyanur Ramachandaran of the University of San Diego in California called the discovery of mirror neurons among the most important of the century and argues that these neurons represent for neuroscience and medicine in general what DNA represent for biology.

Discovered by accident observing the behaviour of monkeys in the laboratory, the Italian researchers have found that there are neurons (in the so-called pre-motor area) that light up when we do actions such as grasping, holding and tearing. Parma researchers noticed that these same neurons are active even when we see others doing those things. This happens even when we see other human beings suffering or feeling emotions such as disgust, anger or happiness. Remember, laughs or yawns are also contagious.

Mirror neurons explain why we tend to replicate and feel the same expressions of other human beings when we see them suffering in an accident or eating disgusting food. Mirror neurons are the basis of learning because they govern the formation of memory. We feel the physical pain when we see it on television when, for example, an athlete is injured; we laugh when others are laughing.

How important is this for the fundraiser? It means that if we can show with images, words or even smells what other human beings feel, we can also activate in our potential donors a part of the brain that will replicate the same feelings. This in turn will activate the pre-motor and decision areas of the brain that could lead, for example, to a potential donor making a donation or becoming active in a cause.

The hormones of a donation: Oxytocin and cortisol. The second discovery that supports and complements mirror neurons comes from neuroscientist and economist Paul Zak.[15] Using MRI, researchers at Parma found that brain areas like pre-motor are reached by an increased inflow of blood when we are moved emotionally. Paul Zak found the same in the blood itself. In fact, Zak has discovered that there are two basic substances or hormones released by the brain in certain situations.

The first is oxytocin, a hormone released by women during childbirth, but also when we feel empathy for others who are suffering. The second is cortisol

---

14. Rizzolatti, Giacomo; Sinigaglia, Corrado (2008). *Mirrors In The Brain: How Our Minds Share Actions and Emotions.* New York: Oxford University.
15. Zack, Paul. *The Moral Molecule: The Source of Love and Prosperity*, Bantam Press, 2012.

(cortisone derivative), which increases in our blood in stressful situations and serves to focus our attention. Zak has spent his life trying, measuring and explaining what happens to chemical levels in our bodies when we feel emotions or compassion for our fellow humans. By measuring the levels of the two hormones in our blood, Zak has discovered that empathy and our propensity to donate depend on the level of certain chemicals (issued or stimulated by the brain) in our blood.[16]

In one experiment, for example, he asked two distinct groups to donate to some causes and organizations after an injection. The first group received a dose of oxytocin, and the second group only a placebo. The result? The first group has proved to be 80 percent more generous in donating not only in general but also in the average gift.

In a second experiment,[17] Zak measured what happens to a group of people watching a very emotional video about a child with brain cancer and its story told by his father. Here's what Zak discovered:

1. Cortisol is a chemical that helps to be more 'attentive, to focus our senses such as sight or hearing. Cortisol is active during stressful situations. Therefore, the more we are stressed, the more we produce cortisol and the more we pay attention to the stimulus we face (a story, an image, etc.).

2. Oxytocin is a hormone linked to empathy that makes us feel connected with others. More oxytocin is released in the blood more we feel "empathetic" for a person (even against a "virtual" person whose story we are told).

Participants in an experiment conducted by Zak were asked, after looking at the video, to donate to a range of organizations that deal with research and assistance to children with cancer. Results? People with the highest level of cortisol and oxytocin were those more inclined to donate. Not only that, the level of oxytocin in the blood can also be used to predict the level of contribution, i.e., how much each person donates to a particular cause or organization. This discovery, Zak says, emphasizes that our brains are hardwired to respond to certain stimuli, especially to the situation of other human beings, through the stories that are told. It also explains that donating to a person, or supporting a cause or an organization, depends on being able to ensure, through the stories, that our brain releases an

---

16. Barraza, J. A.; Zak, P. J. (2009). "Empathy toward Strangers Triggers Oxytocin Release and Subsequent Generosity." *Annals of the New York Academy of Sciences* 1167: 182–189.
17. http://www.youtube.com/watch?v=DHeqQAKHh3M&feature=youtu.be

adequate level of cortisol and oxytocin.

When participants in the experiment see images of the father and son walking hand in hand, no area of the brain is activated because there is nothing on which to focus attention or feel empathy. When the father begins to talk about his son's situation and how he feels knowing that few months of his life has remain, then the mesolimbic system is active and a high level of cortisol and oxytocin are released in the blood. Zak also measured heartbeat, the level of sweating, etc., and got the same results.

Stories and their emotional content, not the creative messages or logo, activate the predisposition to donate.

Giving makes us happy—and more. The latest discovery was made in 2006 by a group of researchers from different universities: Jorge Moll, Frank Krueger, Roland Zahn, Matteo Pardini, Ricardo de Oliveira-Souza, and Jordan Grafman.[18] Using MRI and CT scans, this group found that the mesolimbic system is activated when we make a donation and this is the same area that is activated when we get other rewards like a monetary rewards (for example, winning the lottery or getting a raise) or when we taste our favourite food.

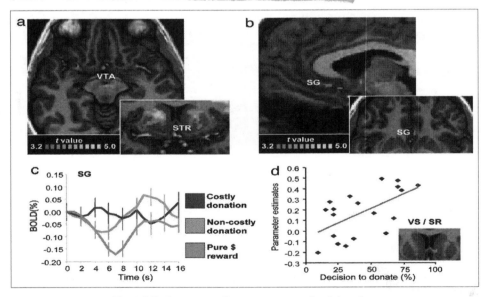

Fig. 1.6. Brain responses for monetary reward and donation.

So the act of giving is not only ignited by specific mechanisms in the brain

---

18. Moll Jorge, Krueger Frank, Zahn Roland, Pardini Matteo, de Oliveira-Souza Ricardo, and Grafman Jordan, "Human fronto–mesolimbic networks guide decisions about charitable donation," http://www.pnas.org/content/103/42/15623.full.pdf+html.

that govern our emotional system and respond to specific emotional sti
donating money to a cause or organization also produces reward mecha
that make us feel happy. This discovery is substantiated with neurophysi
fact, the truth discovered by one of the fathers of the fundraising, Hank Rosso:
Fundraising is the gentle art of teaching others the joy of giving!

Before going into the practical application of these findings in marketing and
fundraising, let's summarize the main elements that neuroscience have helped to
uncover:

- Decisions are triggered by the limbic system, which is in the unconscious
  part of the brain, and which regulates the formation of our memories and
  our heartbeat. The rational part, which governs our logical thinking and
  language, intervenes only after the decision is made (the so-called "gut
  feeling") to justify or explain why we've taken certain actions.
- Our brain works primarily through images: two-thirds of the stimuli that
  reach the brain are visual, and more than half of the brain works on visual
  stimuli.
- A part of our brain is programmed to recognize and react to certain
  stimuli through emotions that trigger chemicals in the blood (oxytocin,
  cortisol, dopamine); these guide our actions and trigger feelings like empathy or the urge to donate to people, causes and social organizations.
- Mirror neurons and oxytocin provide the scientific basis to the fact that
  we feel sympathy and empathy for others who are suffering. And they can
  be used to predict and measure the desire to help when we see someone
  who is suffering or is in trouble because this is programmed in our DNA,
  even when we see the suffering or the difficulties of someone "virtually"
  on TV or through a story.
- The same part of the brain that governs emotions (limbic system) is
  active when we decide to donate, triggering the same reaction and the
  same feelings caused by other stimuli such as sex, food or money, and in
  particular by releasing chemicals that make us feel good when we give or
  help others.

All of the above prove that giving makes us happy.

Neuroscience at the supermarket: Buy an emotion, not a product!

Commercial marketing understood before others the potential of emotions
in influencing consumers to choose a product, a brand or a service. Until a

few years ago, as Henry Ford said, half of the budget spent on advertising was useless; we just do not know which half. Marketers have started to realize that being "on brand" is not as important as previously thought. Neither is the price, the packaging and even the product itself. But what is crucial is to create an emotional connection between the product or brand and the consumer. In fact, if we consider commercial successes of recent years such as Apple, Starbucks or Facebook, we can see that they are not selling the products themselves but the emotional attachment they generate.

Hamish Pringle and Peter Field from the UK Institute of Practitioners in Advertising (IPA),[19] which brings together British advertising agencies, analyzed 1,400 advertising campaigns from the point of view of sales and profits generated. They found that the majority of the successful campaigns were those using emotional content.

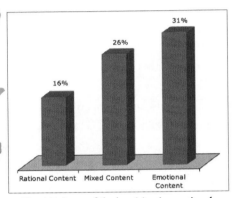

Fig. 1.7. Successful advertising is emotional.

Other research has amply demonstrated the decisive role of emotions in the choices that guide the consumer to prefer a brand or a product. The Journal of Advertising Research, which conducted a study of 23,000 consumers and 240 advertising campaigns, found that emotions are twice as important as the "facts" (i.e., the product itself) in the consumer's decision to buy.

Roger Dooley is the author of the bestseller *Brainfluence*[20] and creator of neurosciencemarketing.com, the most popular site on the use of neuroscience in marketing. He clearly showed that 95 percent of our brain activity happens unconsciously and therefore all marketing strategies should stop targeting the conscious and rational side of the consumer's brain, and use more strategies to address the part

19. Field, Peter and Hamish Pringle. *Brand Immortality: How Brands Can Live Long and Prosper*, IPA, 2008.
20. Dooley, Roger. B*rainfluence: 100 Ways to Persuade and Convince Consumers with Neuromarketing*, John Wiley & Sons, 2011.

of the brain that really decides, and responds to sensory stimuli: the emotions.

Dan Hill, who inspired the idea of this book, has perfected the science of "emotionomics" through applying neuroscience principles to marketing research. Hill founded a company, SensoryLogic, that works to analyze how businesses in general can improve their communication and marketing by better integrating and using emotions.[21] This application of neuroscience in marketing (which we will see in detail in the next chapter) was unprecedented both in commercial marketing and in communications and advertising. The key assumptions of Dan Hill on emotionomics applied to marketing and advertising are as follows:

Impulse buying. An impulse purchase is an unplanned decision to buy a product or service, made just before a purchase. Research findings suggest that emotions and feelings play a decisive role in purchasing, triggered by seeing the product or upon exposure to a well-crafted promotional message. Purchases (or the decision to buy something) are decided by the amygdala—and so are driven by emotions, hence the term "impulsive" buying—and rational explanations to justify why we have purchased a product or a brand only come after, through the rational part of our brain. In fact, how many times after you have seen your credit card bill have you wondered why you bought that thing?

Reputation of the brand. The parts of the brain that recall a product or a brand—which is the purpose of advertising, i.e., that you remember a product or a brand—are the hippocampus and amygdala. This is because the amygdala and the hippocampus are the only two parts of the brain that govern the creation of memory and the triggering of memories when we need to judge a new experience. It's no coincidence they are the same two parts that govern emotions.

A picture is worth a thousand words. Humans act primarily on visual stimuli. Two-thirds of the stimuli that reach the brain are visual; 50 percent of our brain focuses only on handling visual input; and 80 percent of everything we learn is based on visual input.

Hill has identified six key emotions that act everywhere, regardless of race, gender, culture and geographical residence: happiness, surprise, anger, disgust, sadness and fear. Each of these emotions, as shown later, can be at a low or high intensity and trigger reactions and actions of different types. The conclusion derived from the discoveries of neuroscience applied to commercial marketing is unanimous: a campaign or advertising without emotional content will fail to move the audience and therefore will not succeed in terms of market penetration, sales and customer loyalty.

---

21. Hill, Dan. *Emotionomics: Leveraging Emotions for Business Success*, Revised edition, Kogan Page, 2008.

How should business and advertising respond to these neuroscience challenges? By radically changing their communications with the public and how they talk about their brands and products. A clear example that explains how business and marketing are moving from an "on brand" approach to "on emotion" approach is this Michelin advertising line: "Because so much is riding on your tires."

Fig. 1.8. Michelin ad.

Does this campaign work from a rational point of view? Of course not. When is the last time you saw a child inside the tire of a car passing by? This advertisement has nothing to do with the car and its quality, but relies entirely on taking the most valuable and vulnerable thing you have (a child) and placing it inside a tire, creating an emotional connection with the feelings of security and tenderness. And this ad works in terms of market penetration and sales. Dan Hill explains that in the United States, consumers are still willing to pay a little more for Michelin tires.

Much, if not almost all, advertising from the 1990s onwards has gradually moved from brands and products (prices, superiority, package) to the attempt to create an emotional bond with the brand or the product.

Recent examples are the campaigns from Procter and Gamble, Volkswagen and Google.

The Procter and Gamble campaign for the 2012 London Olympics portrays a series of stories dedicated to mothers. The original ad ("Best Job") (http://www.youtube.com/watch?v=soCZcHAfP1Q), lasting two minutes, has been diffused through various social networks and on television. The ad, filmed by the Mexican film director Alejandro Gonzalez Inarritu, is without words and guided by the song "Divenire" by Ludovico Einaudi. The spot shows four mothers who, in four cities of the world (London, Rio De Janeiro, Los Angeles, Beijing), accompany their children to training, day after day, effort after effort, to Olympic success. It is a masterpiece of photography, rhythm, narrative synthesis and musical emotion. And more importantly the ad talks to mothers emotionally as the prime purchasers of their products. Fear, sadness and anger are all mixed very well with joy and happiness that create the final call to action as an emotional peak: "The most challenging job in the world is also the best in the world. Thanks a lot, Mom." The campaign highlights all the moms of Olympic athletes who have made sacrifices to accompany their children to the finish. At the same time this is a tribute to all the mothers of the world, and potential consumers.

Fig. 1.9. P&G ad (Dove).

Fig. 1.10. Volkswagen ad.

The last example is from Google, a commercial for which the company spent $3 million to spread through a multimedia campaign (Google's Parisian Love, http://www.youtube.com/watch?v=rS4Lb-ie4Lc). The spot was produced at zero cost—no actors, no special effects, etc.—and tells a love story through a simple search on Google.

Fig. 1.11. Google ad.

The specialized company Sands Research analyzed the 60 second Google spot broadcast during the American Super Bowl, a program with the largest audience in the U.S. Sands Research measured, using MRI, that the Google ad had the greatest neuro-emotional (neuro-engagement) involvement compared to any other ads that year during Super Bowl. The spot solicited the highest activation of those areas of the brain that govern emotions and hence also delivered an increase in users and advertising sales.

The trend of using emotions in advertising is even more evident in the Super Bowl ads from 2013 onwards. To give you an idea of the importance in getting these spots right, a 30-second spot during the Super Bowl costs $4 million. In this context, Sands Research found that those commercials with the highest level of emotional engagement measured through MRI according to the Sands Research model are also those delivering more sales afterwards.

2013 Super Bowl Ad Rankings

CocaCola Security Cameras	7.00
Budweiser Clydesdales	7.00
Bud Light Journey	6.97
Kia Sorento Space Babies	6.83
Taco Bell Viva Young	6.54
Ram Trucks Farmer	6.33
Fast and the Furious 6	6.32
Bud Light Lucky Chair	6.29
Samsung Mobile USA The Next Big Thing	6.04
Fiat 500 Cabrio Topless	5.86
Audi Prom	5.74
Subway 15 Years	5.56
Best Buy Asking Amy	5.54
Calvin Klein	5.10
Coke Chase	5.04
Lincoln MKS Phoenix	4.91
Pepsi Next Party	4.75
Kia Forte Hotbots	4.73
Speed Stick Unattended Laundry	4.72
Doritos Goat 4 Sale	4.71

Fig. 1.12. Sands Research of Super Bowl ads.

Coca Cola, which uses security cameras to show acts of kindness and philanthropy (http://www.youtube.com/watch?v=ceTBF1Hik5I&nofeather=True), and Budweiser, with its story of a horse and its trainer from birth until the day they meet again after many years (http://www.youtube.com/watch?v=wPG7PcI67dE), or with the puppy, are good examples. They had the best neuro-engagement score and delivered the best sales.

For those who are interested in the methodology and the classification of the various spots at Super Bowl they can go to the web site http://www.sandsresearch.com/2013AdRankings.aspx where every year the TV spots in the Super Bowl are measured and analyzed.

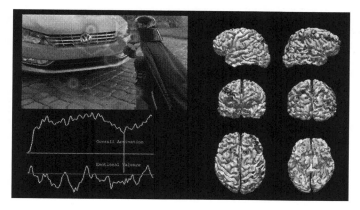

Fig. 1.13. Brain activation during Super Bowl spot according to Sands Research.

And if you think that emotional response and drive are limited to the Western world, you may consider the campaign and ads from a Thai company, Thai Life Insurance, The Unsung Hero (https://www.youtube.com/watch?v=uaWA2GbcnJU).

Fig. 1.14. The Unsung Hero.

This campaign not only has recorded 29 million+ views on Youtube and driven the company's best sales, it has also generated a number of reactions of people filming themselves while watching the video and showing what they prove.

Fig. 1.15. Reactions to the Thai Life Insurance spot.

Chapter 2

You can call this emotion:
How our brain works
when we decide to
support a cause or an organization

The science of emotions and fundraising

If neuroscience pioneered a revolution, especially in psychology, economics and marketing, these findings substantially affect (or should in the near future) the way we do fundraising. For a long time many professional fundraisers and those involved in non-profit organizations imagined and believed that it was necessary to create an emotional connection between the cause, the organization, the mission and the donors.

In fact, the classic pattern of a fundraising campaign (a letter, a spot or a website, but also a speech during a face to face meeting with a donor) should contain and clearly show the following elements:

a) The need or problem. This should contain emotional aspects such as sadness, anger, fear, surprise.

b) The answer or solution. This should convey positive emotions associated with happiness and feeling good, through the possible answer to the need or problem presented.

c) A request for a donation. This supports the solution presented to alleviate/save/cure/improve/fix/stop the need or the problem.

Adrian Sargeant[22] has found the origins of this scheme of fundraising in a 14th-century book that provides 22 types of letters monks in England used to raise funds. According to this scheme, which is still the one adopted by many nonprofit organizations, at the beginning there is an introduction with a mellifluous

---

22. Sargeant, A. and Jay, E. (2004), *Fundraising Management: Analysis, Planning and Practice,* Routledge, London.

You can Fix the problem by giving through us!

greeting, a tactical introduction, a description of the problem, a petition (or "call to action") and a final enthusiastic conclusion. This scheme has proven to work in fundraising, especially in direct mail, even if, as Sergeant noticed[23], so far there has been little interest in the academic world to confirm its scientific efficacy or the theoretical foundations of this scheme.

The truth is that the way we convey, express or represent each of these parts—the need or the solution, the request or the appeal—through words and images, has been so far very intuitive. We can say it has been sometimes creative, based on experience and often left to the imagination of the advertising agencies, which in many cases have purely commercial training and experience that doesn't always suit the non-profit world.

What emotions and what images work better in fundraising is a very controversial subject. In fact, both inside and outside the non-profit world there is an endless debate about whether it is appropriate to ban or to reduce the use of certain images perceived as too strong. There is also discussion around how appropriate it is to use only positive images instead of those characterized as "tearjerkers."

Ethical discussions on the use of certain images, and the use of mechanisms to activate specific emotions, will be discussed in a separate chapter. However, the theme of this chapter is how non-profit organizations and fundraisers can better use neuroscience effectively to convince and influence more supporters and donors.

Among the few fundraisers who understood the impact and applications of neuroscience revolution for fundraising are Ken Burnett,[24] one of the fathers of relational fundraising, and Tom Ahern, one of the American gurus of communications for nonprofits.

Burnett, who by his own admission has discovered the potential of emotional fundraising only recently, argued that the findings of neuroscience represent for fundraisers both a treasure and a Pandora's box.

"Can fundraising really be so predictably easy?" asks Burnett. "Well, yes, it can, if we understand our donors' emotional brains and find ways to consistently and indelibly print powerful, emotional, appropriate memories there, to be reactivated later. First impressions last. Sure they do.

23. Merchant A., Ford J.B and Sargeant A. (2010). "Charitable Organizations' Storytelling Influence on Donors' Emotions and Intentions," *Journal of Business Research*, 63 (2010), pages 754-762.
24. Burnett, Ken. "The Emotional Brain. Effective fundraising, it seems, is all in the mind," http://www.sofii.org/node/1004

This is a transformational insight, the single biggest realization of all. It explains things that many fundraisers often feel intuitively but mostly haven't quite rationalized and that others miss altogether. Such as the surge of emotion when we see a child in distress, the appeal in the direct gaze of a child's eyes that means all we have to say is, "sponsor me"; no more explanation is needed. Or the sweating palms and lump in the throat conjured by the mere image of those soldiers in First World War trenches, waiting for that whistle. Or the recall of time, place and feelings prompted by a piece of music from our past, or by the smell of perfume, or the taste of an exotic fruit. Think Amnesty's long copy ads, children running from exploding shells, or waiting in food queues at times of famine, or the tired, shocked, dripping life boatman just washed in from the sea.

How powerful are the emotions conjured by images such as these? How useful would it be to consistently harness them to your cause? Well, the emotional scenes are already there or they can be planted there to be called upon later, if only we get better at emotional storytelling, at presenting our emotional case with power and passion that will burn the memory of our story so deep that it will last and last long term, to be called upon again and again, whenever needed.

We should study the brain to learn how we can skillfully, sensitively and carefully exploit its potential to store emotional memories that we can access, later, when we have use for them."

Tom Ahern in 2011[25] has clearly explained that neuroscience is, for fundraisers, the most important trend in the coming years. "The old dualistic concept that emotions and reason are in constant conflict to control the life of a human being is the wrong approach," says Ahern. Emotions govern our choices. The implications for fundraising are obvious: we do not have to try to reason with people to give money to us. We must try to engage with their emotions. To paraphrase the Canadian neurologist Donald Calne, reason leads to thinking, while emotion leads to action.[26] In fundraising, the action of giving is usually our goal. As a fundraiser, said Ahem, we do not care much if people think about our cause. We care more that our cause generates enough excitement for someone who

---

25. Ahern,Tom. "12.03: The Brain According to Me. Neuroscience is the most important force at work in fundraising today. Or it should be." http://www.aherncomm.com/ss_plugins/content/content.php?content 5094
26. Calne, David. *Within Reason: Rationality and Human Behavior*, Vintage; Reprint edition, 2000.

wants to help and make a donation. The idea of "educating" people to become our supporters, concludes Ahern, puts too much emphasis on a rational analysis and statistical element. In fact—and this is fascinating—the more you try to introduce the reason (facts and figures), the less money you raise.

The six key emotions and Emotionmeter

Based on major findings from neuroscience, in particular the work of Paul Ekman, Dan Hill[27] has managed to synthesize the key emotions that drive our decisions and our actions, and then the marketing strategies needed to adapt to this new paradigm.

First, based on Hill and Ekman, let us define emotions, a term that is likely to be left too broad or based on intuitive interpretations. Emotions have four universal characteristics:

a) **A perceptual component** that includes physical sensations and chemical changes in the brain and is activated in our body from the brain (via, for example, the release of hormones in the blood such as oxytocin, cortisol, etc.);

b) **A reflective component**, through a conscious or intuitive thinking that is activated in response to sensory stimuli;

c) **A behavioural component**, through expressive reactions on our face (such as smiling or crying) and with specific actions (I have to run or fight?);

d) **A sensory component**, such as images, sounds, etc., that trigger an emotional response.

Hill has identified six key emotions:[28]

- Happiness
- Surprise
- Anger
- Disgust
- Sadness
- Fear

---

27. Hill, Dan. *Emotionomics: Leveraging emotions for business success*, Revised edition. Kogan Page, 2008; Dan Hill, *About Face: The secrets of emotionally effective advertising*. Kogan Page, 2010.

28. Hill and Ekman have identified seven key emotions, including "contempt," which is less physical —and more attitudinal—than disgust. However, for classification and practical purposes, here it is summarized as more primary disgust.

The six key emotions as identified by Hill and Ekman can be imagined as a spectrum: they can be high intensity or low intensity. For example, we can feel pain (high intensity) or just be sad (low intensity), or we may feel annoyed (low intensity) or be angry (high Intensity). This is very clear in the Atlas of Emotion developed by Ekman and mentioned earlier.

Atlas of Emotions: Sadness

STATES OF SADNESS

Each emotion contains a number of related states, which differ in intensity. The states shown here are representative, not exhaustive.

ANGUISH
SORROW
GRIEF
DESPAIR
MISERY
HOPELESSNESS
HELPLESSNESS
RESIGNATION
DISTRAUGHTNESS
DISCOURAGEMENT
DISAPPOINTMENT

LEAST INTENSE   MOST INTENSE

Emotionmeter©

JOY	AMAZEMENT	RAGE	LOATHING	GRIEF	TERROR
Happiness	Surprise	Anger	Disgust	Sadness	Fear
Satisfaction	Curiosity	Annoyance	Boredom	Pensiveness	Worry

HIGH INTENSITY EMOTIONS/low intensity emotions
Adapted from Hill and Ekman

Fig. 2.16. States of sadness and intensity, according to Ekman and The Emotionmeter©.

In the *Emotionmeter* I summarized the emotion spectrum using the classification of Hill so that six key emotions are aligned along the spectrum of intensity, low or high.

What is important about this tool is that it shows how emotions are positioned in a spectrum that ranges from a low intensity to a high intensity, and each one ignites a type of reaction and action, depending on their intensity and combination. For example, some images, words or sounds can only generate a feeling of general discomfort, but do not make us angry enough to take an initiative (i.e., bang a fist on the table). A message or an image can leave us so amazed, terrified or in pain as to make us feel stuck or paralyzed, and unable to do anything and therefore unable to make any decision or take action. Finding the right emotional level is crucial for our fundraising and for our target.

The second consideration is that the six key emotions are like the primary colours (yellow, red, blue). As with colours, we mix them to produce other colours like purple or orange, to create a full range of emotions. By combining the different possibilities, Dan Hill has provided a more comprehensive framework for primary and secondary emotions. What is important is that these emotions are all located in specific areas of the brain that are active and ignite chemical and physical actions. Therefore, these are not theoretical insights or arbitrary classifications of feelings, but biological and chemical measurements of where and how our emotions are formed and activated in our brain.

	SURPRISE	ANGER	DISGUST	SADNESS	FEAR
HAPPINESS	*Admiration Relief*	*Pride* **Revenge**	**Morbidity**	*Greed Nostalgia*	*Hope* **Guilt**
	SURPRISE	**Indignation**		**Embarrassment Disappointment**	**Awe Alarm**
		ANGER	**Contempt Scorn**	**Bitterness Envy**	**Jealousy**
			DISGUST	**Regret**	**Shame Prudery**
				SADNESS	**Despair Distress**

Positive Emotions
Negative Emotions

Fig. 2.17. Negative and positive emotions.

As you can see, only six of the 30 emotions are positive (Admiration, Relief, Pride, Greed, Hope, Nostalgia) while most are negative. We will discuss further the reasons and causes of the prevalence of negative emotions. According to Dan Hill, this is due to the evolution of our brain (and indeed, as we have seen, the mesolimbic system is among the most ancient parts of our brain). The increased susceptibility to negative emotions derives from the need for survival of the species, and therefore the need to have a greater number of tools to react to events and negative situations that can help us to decide whether, for example, when faced with danger we escape or fight.

Negative emotions are overwhelming and sometimes more effective than others, even in fundraising. Deborah Small and Nicole Verocchi of the Wharton School of the University of Pennsylvania[29] have shown in some experiments that negative images stimulate or attract many more donations than neutral or positive images. According to this study, people give more if there is a photograph with the face of a sad child. One group of participants received $10 and some fundraising letters from organizations involved in cancer research. Participants received three letters: one with the image of a happy child, one with a photograph of a child with a neutral expression and a third one with the image of a sad-looking child. Results? The letter with a sad picture got major donations.

Each of the emotions, as already explained, activates or stimulates reactions and specific actions, among which there may be actions like buying a product, making a donation and signing a petition. The table shows the main reactions and behaviours triggered by different emotions.

Mean Donations by Emotion Expression in Study 1

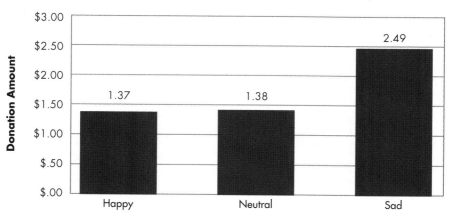

Fig. 2.18. Donations triggered by emotions (D. Small, N. Verocchi, 2009).

Each emotion triggers different states in terms of level of attention, type of

29. Small, D. and N. Verocchi. "The Face of Need: Facial Emotion. Expression on Charity Advertisements," *Journal of Marketing Research*, Vol. XLVI (December 2009), 777-787.

action and speed in making a decision. For example, if what we seek is to draw attention to our message, we should focus on positive emotions such as happiness or surprise; focusing only on fear or disgust can generate less attention.

		EMOTIONAL PRIMARY STATES					
		HAPPINESS	SURPRISE	ANGER	FEAR	SADNESS	DISGUST
BEHAVIOURAL OUTCOMES	Results orientation	**HIGH** focus on reward	Indecision between reward and punishment	**HIGH** focus on reward	Indecision between reward and punishment	**HIGH** focus on reward	**HIGH** focus on punishment avoidance
	Attention level	**HIGH**	**HIGH**	**MEDIUM**	**MEDIUM**	**HIGH**	**LOW**
	Possibility of action	**HIGH** search for outcomes	**HIGH** search for outcomes	**HIGH** fight or flight	**LOW** delay, paralysis	**LOW** delay, paralysis	**HIGH** focus on prevention
	Decision	**FAST**	**CAUTIOUS** (uncertain)	**FAST** (impulsive)	**CAUTIOUS** (uncertain)	**CAUTIOUS** (uncertain)	**FAST**

Fig. 2.19. Emotions, decisions and actions.

If, however, what we want is quick and instant action, then we should focus more on emotions such as happiness, surprise or anger. Finally, if, for example, we want someone to send an SMS or call a phone number, we should focus more on making feel people happy, angry or disgusted so that we can have a more rapid response than if we make them feel surprised, frightened or sad; chances are, that would make them feel helpless or paralyzed.

As we have seen in the previous chart, there is no single emotion formula that ensures greater attention or a more effective response to our appeals and campaigns. Emotions are a puzzle, and only the correct combination, depending on your cause and the audience you wish to reach, adequately tested, can indicate which works best.

In fundraising, emotions are critical for various reasons:

1. Emotions guide our decisions in general and when we donate. As fundraisers we have to be able to stir up the right emotions and create an emotional connection between our cause and the donor.

2. Giving makes someone happy. This positive emotion, instigated by the gesture of donating money to a cause or to a project, is what we must aspire to—and, in a long-term relationship with donors, we must try to maintain the same level of happiness after the donation.

3. Emotions are not neutral but a powerful force that push us to perform an action. Each of the key emotions or the combination of them results in actions, which for us could be making a donation, sponsoring a child or a monument, joining a campaign, mobilizing our friends, and so on.

4. Of the six key emotions and the 30 arising from their mix, most are negative. This is not a value judgment, but the result of the evolution of our brain that originally needed more information and options to recognize and react to negative events. This also does not mean that our communications and our fundraising should always be led by negative emotions. On the contrary, the right mix of positive and negative emotions is necessary, and also depends on the type of results we seek: attention to our message; an action; or speed of the response to our appeal.

5. Emotions exist on a spectrum or range from a low to high intensity. Knowing how to find the right emotional level is the task of fundraising organizations, and non-profit organizations in general. An emotional level that's too low could mean your message goes unnoticed or produces little engagement among target audiences, generating no actions or limited donations. A too-high emotional level could simply cause paralysis in the audience or generate a negative reaction—including the refusal to participate in or donate to your appeal.

Chapter 3

Emotions at work:
Why do some campaigns
raise more money than others?

The Fiona and Rachel emotions

How do emotions work in fundraising? In the second part of the book we will analyze various examples of emotions in fundraising campaigns. We will also try to understand how the various sensory stimuli (images, sounds, words, etc.) can play a key role in activating one or more emotions.

For now, we will analyze how the six emotions work in practice, with two successful examples from two U.S.-based organizations: Hope for Paws (which helps abandoned animals in Los Angeles) and charity: water, which supports drinking water in developing countries.

These two campaigns, and in particular the videos, work not only because millions of people have seen them[30] and donated after seeing them. They also work because they bring the audiences to tears and smiles. I have shown them to thousands of people around the world, and even among an audience composed of people from different cultures (including participants from less overtly emotional and demonstrative cultures such as the Scandinavian and Asian countries), they provoked the same emotional reaction.

Fig. 3.20. Fiona and Rachel.

---

30. "Charity's video racks up more than a half a million views," http://www.prdaily.com/Main/Articles/13580.aspx#

The following table shows how emotions work in these two campaigns. Before you read the table, or read any further, please watch the two videos (and maybe have some tissues ready!). Here are the links:

Fiona: http://www.youtube.com/watch?v=YJkZXh9v_i4

Rachel: http://www.youtube.com/watch?v=nC_vXAF-pBM

Caution: Even if you do not like animals or children, I guarantee that while you are watching these videos, you will want to cry and smile; you will feel upset; and you will get goosebumps.

The first, "Fiona," tells the story of a dog abandoned on the outskirts of Los Angeles and found by the Hope for Paws volunteers. They discover that Fiona, besides being abandoned, is also blind. Volunteers with the help of a vet can restore the vision in one eye, and Fiona can see for the first time. She is then adopted.

The second, "Rachel," is the story of a 9-year-old girl who decided to use her birthday to raise funds to get drinking water for an Ethiopian village. Unfortunately, she raised only $220 of her $300 target before she was tragically killed a month later in a car accident. Her story inspired so many people that the charity called charity: water raised over $2 million by people inspired by Rachel.

Let's take a look at the emotions in these two examples.

ANGER	SURPRISE	DISGUST	SADNESS	FEAR	HAPPINESS
Fiona is blind and defenceless, abandoned in the dump. Rachel wanted to raise $300 for her birthday so that 15 people could have clean water, but fell a little short, raising $220. She tells her mother she would try harder next time. A month later, she dies in a car accident.	A doctor can restore the sight in one of Fiona's eyes. The shock of Rachel's death. Rachel's mother's smile when she sees water from the well.	Fiona urinates out of fear and sits on it, frozen. Fiona has the worst flea infestation the charity workers have ever seen.	Fiona had not only been abandoned but was also blind in both eyes. A brave girl, who was just 9 and raising money for others, is killed in a tragic accident. The first part of the charity:water video is about remembering and honouring Rachel.	The charity workers realize Fiona is blind, so they allow her to smell them. Fiona is terrified, as are the charity workers.	Fiona's tail is wagging and she is running around happily after her eye operation. The second part of the charity: water video shows the happy faces of children dancing, and Rachel's parents smiling.

Fig 3.21. Emotions elicited in the spot Fiona and Rachel.

In the two examples, there is a very well balanced use of various emotions, and therefore they have success in terms of online views, sharing and donations. They have a nice mix of images, music, sounds, spoken words and texts. These two examples also help us to learn how different emotions are activated and to identify and clarify some key principles of Emotionraising, which will be presented in the second part of the book.

These are the principles of Emotionraising that we will see through various success stories:

- One against all: The power of the individual vs. statistics.
- Once upon a time: The role of stories and storytelling.
- Empire of fundraising senses: Sights, sounds, touch, smells and words.
- In good and evil: The power of positive and negative emotions.

One against all: The power of the individual vs. statistics

The two examples from Hope for Paws and charity: water exemplify clearly one of the key elements for the activation of emotions: in both cases it's a specific story, a dog (Fiona) and a girl (Rachel). Think about the difference and impact the two campaigns would have if, rather than relying on the two stories, they were focused on statistics to explain the abandonment of animals or the lack of drinking water in Africa.

For example, surely the outcome would not have been the same if instead of Fiona's story the organization used statistics such as the following: "The number of abandoned dogs in L.A. has grown by 60 percent, and 40,595 animals were abandoned last year. Abuse towards animals grew by 23.5 percent last year."

In the words of Mother Teresa of Calcutta: "If I look at the mass of people I will never act, but if I look at the story of a single person, I will." The fact that our brains are programmed to pay attention and then empathize and help (or donate to help) individuals (or people, animals, monuments, schools, etc.), rather than to pay attention to abstract statistics or groups, was proven by various studies. One in particular was conducted by Deborah Small and George Lowenstein from the University of Pittsburg[31] and summarized by Paul Slovic.[32] In this experiment on generosity, participants were asked to donate to Save the Children (all or a portion

---

31. Small, D. A.; Loewenstein, G.; and Slovic, P. (2007). "Sympathy and Callousness: The impact of deliberative thought on donations to identifiable and statistical victims." *Organizational Behavior and Human Decision Processes*, Volume 102, pages 143-153.

32. Slovic, Paul. "If I look at the mass I will never act. Psychic numbing and genocide," *Judgment and Decision Making*, Vol. 2, No. 2, April 2007, pp. 79-95.; Deborah A. Small, George Loewenstein, Paul Slovic. "To Increase Charitable Donations, Appeal to the Heart — Not the Head." *Organizational Behavior and Human Decision Processes*, Volume 102, Issue 2, March 2007, pages 143–153.

of the $5 they had received). The participants were divided into three groups:

- The first group was given an accurate and detailed description of an emergency situation in Africa with statistics like, "The shortage of food in Malawi affects more than 3 million children" and "More than 11 million people in Ethiopia need food aid immediately."

- The second group received the story of a little girl. "All donations go to help Rokia, a 7-year-old girl from Mali. Rokia is very poor, and is at risk of severe malnutrition or even death due to lack of food."

- The third group received a mix of the two examples.

Statistical Lives

- Food shortages in Malawi are affecting more than 3 million children.

- In Zambia, severe rainfall deficits have resulted in a 42 percent drop in maize production from 2000. As a result, an estimated 3 million Zambians face hunger.

- Four million Angolans — one third of the population — have been forced to flee their homes.

- More than 11 million people in Ethiopia need immediate food assistance.

Identifiable Lives

Any money that you donate will go to Rokia, a 7-year-old girl from Mali, Africa. Rokia is desperately poor, and faces a threat of severe hunger or even starvation. Her life will be changed for the better as a result of your financial gift. With your support, and the support of other caring sponsors, Save the Children will work with Rokia's family and other members of the community to help feed her, provide her with education, as well as basic medical care and hygiene education.

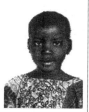

Fig. 3.22. Examples provided in the test by Deborah Small and George Lowenstein.

The result? The story of Rokia got the highest donations, an average of $2.50, about half of the total compensation received, while those who received only the statistical information donated the least, an average of $1.14.

Psychologists have identified this mechanism they call "mental and physical paralysis"[33] as the phenomenon whereby individuals gradually become insensitive to the dimension of human suffering. For example, while there is a strong increase in empathy when the number of those suffering goes from zero to one (an individual), there is a gradual decrease in empathy when moving from one victim to two, three and so on. Moreover, when the number of those suffering becomes exceptionally large—as in the case of genocide, famine, etc.—the emotions of

---

33. Slovic, Paul, Baruch Fischhoff, and Sarah Lichtenstein. (1980). "Facts and Fears: Understanding Perceived Risk." In Richard C. Schwing and Walther A. Alberts, Jr. (eds.), *Societal Risk Assessment: How Safe is Safe Enough?* New York: Plenum Press.

sympathy and empathy decrease to the point that people react less emotionally to mass suffering situations than to more circumscribed situations.

This response mechanism to the stories of individuals rather than the statistics has been used over the years by many organizations and many successful fundraisers.

1. Amnesty International (AI) was founded precisely to defend the rights of two Portuguese individuals and, to this day, AI still bases most of its actions, including fundraising, on mobilizing its supporters to appeal or campaign for specific cases of people and individuals unjustly imprisoned. This makes it an extremely compelling cause to support.

Fig. 3.23. The first article about two Portuguese prisoners was the origin of Amnesty International.

2. Humanitarian organizations have developed child sponsorship (for instance, Save the Children, World Vision and that Action Aid to name a few) as a mechanism to suggest that you can help a specific child, the child's family or his or her community.

Fig. 3.24. Example of child sponsorship.

3. The idea of the adoption or sponsorship has been used by many more causes: animals, environment, cultural heritage, schools, etc. Each of these initiatives utilizes the idea of helping an "individual beneficiary" or adopting it, rather than supporting generic issues.

Fig. 3.25. Examples of adoption: Animals and villages.

4. Finally, thanks to the new digital technologies, you can support causes and individuals in a more sophisticated way, such as lending money to them via micro-credit as in the case of organizations like KIVA. The loans are intended to go directly to individuals and a donor can check the progress or receive real-time information, both on loan repayments, and how they have been used.

Fig. 3.26. KIVA microloans.

> ## ADVICE AND PRACTICAL TOOLS
>
> The impact and effectiveness of emotionraising depends on the ability to focus our communications on the condition and the problem of an individual or a single beneficiary—a museum, an animal, a school, etc.— who can exemplify issues for which the funds are raised. In fact, our brains are programmed to pay more attention to, and thus empathize more (and potentially then donate) with, the problems and stories of an individual rather than statistics or groups.

Once upon a time: The role of stories and storytelling

The second principle that emerges from the two examples of Rachel and Fiona, and in general from successful fundraising, is that we feel emotions, and therefore we act, when we hear a story.

Following the evolutionarily path of our species and our brains, we are programmed to listen to stories, to narrate them and, through this mechanism, learn, store and enrich our action options to use in various situations.

In a fascinating book by Jonathan Gottschall,[34] who cites various studies and experiments in neuroscience, Gottschall explains that a "daydream" last about 14 seconds on average and we have two thousand of them a day. In other words, we spend half of the time while we are awake and a third of our lives in general imagining and fantasizing. We dream with open eyes about the past (what we could have said or done, we relive failures and successes). We imagine how our life and our work could be different. However, we fantasize more intensely—in Hollywood style— when we sleep, creating stories. We write the script for a movie with a happy conclusion in our minds, but we also create horror stories where our worst fears come true.

Why are stories so much more important than statistics, numbers or figures? Because they are the only way to ensure that our ideas are understood and digested by those who are listening. A team of Princeton researchers[35] observed through CT scans what happens in the brain of the storyteller and that of the listener, and found that the same areas of neurons are activated or "lit up" in

34. Gotschall, Jonathan. *The Storytelling Animal: How Stories Make us Human*, Houghton Mifflin Harcourt, 2012.
35. Stephens G.J.; Silbert L.J.; Hasson U. "Speaker-listener neural coupling underlies successful communication." Proc Natl Acad Sci U.S.A., Aug. 10, 2010; 107(32):14425-30.

both. Therefore, when we tell a story, those who are listening are literally in our minds!

Paul Zak,[36] who discovered oxytocin and how empathy is programmed in our brain (and has been experimenting in the laboratory), explains that neuro-chemicals are released by our brain when emotions are triggered by stories. In an experiment, Zak measured reactions to a video of the St. Jude Children's Research Hospital that tells the story of Ben, a child suffering from a rare form of brain tumour (http://www.youtube. com / watch? v = IhuE8K25TWA). Zak found that the production of oxytocin (empathy) and cortisol (attention) exactly follow the course of the story told by Ben's father: there is a crescendo of cortisol when the story becomes more dramatic, and the most oxytocin is released when he tells what the loss of Ben will mean to him.

Gustav Freytag, a German writer and playwright who reconstructed the structure of a story (see the graph) explains that a story has a precise structure. It starts by illustrating the challenge or problem, gradually grows in intensity until it reaches the climax (a struggle, the risk of death, etc.) and then slowly dissolves in an action that ends positively or dramatically but with lower emotion (denouement). Paul Zak saw that our brain releases substances like cortisol and oxytocin following exactly the ac sequence Freytag describes. For example, while you see the images of Ben and his father in the zoo strolling calmly, nothing happens in our brain because there is nothing to watch. Nevertheless, when the father begins to describe how it feels knowing that Ben has only a few weeks or months to live, then the brain of the listener becomes active, releasing massive doses of oxytocin and cortisol.

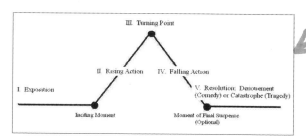

Fig. 3.27. Freytag's diagram.

36. Zack, Paul. *The Moral Molecule: The Source of Love and Propserity*, Bantam Press, 2012.

Peter Gueber,[37] who has been CEO of companies such as Sony and Polygram and producer of films such as *Midnight Express*, *Batman* and *Rain Man*, wrote a bestseller, *Tell to Win*, on how stories and storytelling are the key elements for a successful business. Gueber clearly says that, based on his experience, for any brand or organization to succeed it must be able to tell the right story, one that moves and convinces customers and investors. According to Gueber, a story that works must have a "call to action" clearly defined, and must not end unless there is a clear invitation to the audience to do something. The structure of a story that works for Gueber is the following:

a) A beginning that highlights the problem or the challenge;

b) A middle that includes the difficulties or the struggle that the protagonist or protagonists face;

c) An end, with a solution that inflames the audience and acts as a call to action for what you can, or have to, do.

Merchant, Ford and Sergeant[38] have made clear that fundraising stories should present and involve the donor in an unresolved and unbalanced situation, with an obstacle and a problem to solve. This state is defined as "incident instigator" and serves to focus the attention on the problem and on the protagonist (or hero) to create an emotional connection between the listener and the protagonist. Then the story should invite the listener to take the initiative, letting the listener know how to make a donation or become a supporter in order to resolve this situation. Finally, there should be some lesson or moral learned thanks to this story, a piece where the listener hears or understands that the goal has been reached or the problem has been resolved. This also explains why it is so important to give feedback to donors after donation.

Another way to use the power of stories comes from Jeff Brooks, who gives the example of George Bailey, the protagonist of the famous film *It's a Wonderful Life*, directed by Frank Capra and starring James Stewart. In the movie, an angel gives George Bailey the possibility to see his life as if he had never existed, and only then does he realize the force for good that he has been and how important he is in the lives of many people and his community.[39]

---

37. Guber, Peter. *Tell to Win: Connect, Persuade, and Triumph with the Hidden Power of Story*, Crown Business, 2011.
38. Merchant A.; Ford J.B.; and Sergeant, A. (2010): "Charitable Organizations' Storytelling Influence on Donors' Emotions and Intentions." Journal of Business Research, 63 (2010), pages 754-762.
39. Brooks, Jeff. "Show donors the world without their giving," http://www.futurefundraisingnow.com/future-fundraising/2011/01/show-donors-the-world-without-their-giving.html

This phenomenon, called "counterfactual thinking," is when we think about how life would be if we (or our organization, or our family) had never existed.

Inviting people to think or to imagine the world without his/her own country or without his/her own company results in more attachment, both in terms of patriotic spirit or loyalty as an employee. An application for fundraising, writes Jeff Brooks, could be to show donors how life would be without their donations or let them see the world as if our organization never existed. One application of this principle, as in the example of ActionAid provided here, is to show the impact of donations through testimonials from the beneficiaries or from their field workers. In this case, the story is that without Action Aid, a school will be closed.

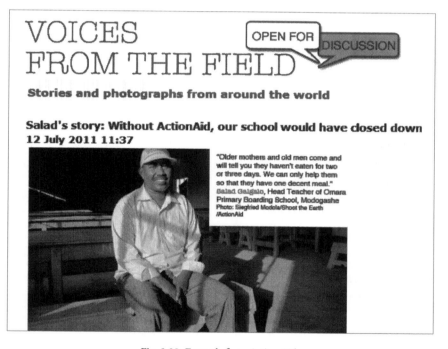

VOICES FROM THE FIELD
OPEN FOR DISCUSSION

Stories and photographs from around the world

Salad's story: Without ActionAid, our school would have closed down
12 July 2011 11:37

"Older mothers and old men come and will tell you they haven't eaten for two or three days. We can only help them so that they have one decent meal."
Salad Galgalo, Head Teacher of Omara Primary Boarding School, Modogashe
Photo: Siegfried Modola/Shoot the Earth /ActionAid

Fig. 3.28. Example from Action Aid.

One of the elements of success of the two stories presented earlier (Fiona and Rachel) is that they contain the key elements to activate emotions: they show both a problem and the difficulties a protagonist faces in overcoming an obstacle. Fiona is blind and abandoned while Rachel died without fulfilling her dream of collecting $300. They have a finale with the solution and a call to action that inspires you to do something like give, share, etc.

ADVICE AND PRACTICAL TOOLS

Humans are a species that evolved in part thanks to stories. Our brain is active when we hear or visualize a story. The success of fundraising — from both the general public and from major donors — depends on the ability to tell stories that harness emotions and lead the listener towards a call to action. A story should have a beginning that exemplifies the dramatic nature of the situation/problem, a middle that describes the difficulty of solving the problem and an end with a solution and "call to action" that invites listeners to donate and support a cause.

Empire of the fundraising senses: Images, sounds, smells, objects and words

As we saw in the first chapter, a combination of sensory elements triggers emotions and therefore our decisions. First, we are moved by what we see, but subsequently also from what we hear, what we smell and what we touch. According to Dan Hill, our senses absorb 400 million bytes of information per second! Therefore, our communication and our fundraising should always try to involve all five senses, because specific parts of our brains are designed to react to different sensory stimuli and trigger specific emotions that in turn activate our attention and guide our involvement towards messages, causes, organizations and events.

The examples of Rachel and Fiona use many sensory stimuli, mainly images and sounds, but also through the written words that stimulate the listeners to imagine smells (for example, the fact that Fiona urinates on herself) or objects that we can almost touch (the gush of water).

Pictures

The visual part of our brain is the most important:
- Two-thirds of the stimuli that reach the brain are visual.
- Over 50% of our brain's focus is to manage visual stimuli.
- 80% of everything we learn is through visual stimuli.
- 55% of communication is derived from facial expressions; 38% from tone of voice; and only 7% from verbal communication—words as they are spoken. (Note that these percentages, identified by Albert Mehrabian, should be considered with caution because they are attributed only when someone expresses opinions on feelings.)

Through neuroscience and the practice of fundraising, we know that a picture is worth more than a thousand words: more images activate areas of our brain, in particular those connected with emotions and the desire to help and give to others.

- We pay more attention and feel more involved with dynamic images, in which a subject is moving, rather than with a static entity—such as subjects sitting or standing—or a written slogan and a logo. That's why if you want a call to action, ensure it has a blank or black screen and text.

- Images become faster as they reach the sensory and emotional part of our brain. While we are able to read 250-300 words per minute on average, an image comes to the sensory part of the brain in 2 milliseconds!

- The emotional part of the brain is more active when we see individuals (babies, animals, etc.) instead of groups, landscapes, objects, etc.

- The level of oxytocin (with the consequent empathy) grows when we see small beings (babies, puppies, etc.).[40] This is also true for those without children or those who say they do not love children and animals. The reason for this is the evolutionary mechanisms, as discovered by Konrad Lorenz, to ensure the survival of the small; the helpless attract more attention.

Evoking images through written words, particularly with the use of the adjectives, activates in the brain similar emotional responses to those we feel when we see the images expressed by words.

Dan Hill has a map to help us identify the most important elements for the use of still images (photographs, web pages, etc.) in marketing and fundraising in order to elicit a more emotional response.

1. **At the centre.** The most important image should always be the focus of our communication and should be big, central and prominent. Our brain, which is efficient, likes to be driven: a central image is perceived better and faster than one positioned on one side, high or low.

2. **Faces.** As we have already pointed out, a face consistently attracts more attention than any other image.

3. **Motion.** Our visual system is programmed to pay attention to motion —say, of a human being, animal or machine—rather than to inanimate objects and subjects.

40. Hendrie, Doug. "The Science of Cute," August 15, 2012, http://www.gizmag.com/the-science-of-cute/23707/; Cara Santa Maria, "The Science Of Cute: Is Pedomorphism Why We Gush Over 'Adorable' Things?" http://www.huffingtonpost.com/2012/11/26/science-of-cute_n_2171987.html?utm_hp_ref=talk-nerdy-to-me&ncid=edlinkusaolp00000008

4. **Size.** The bigger the size of an image, the higher the chance it has to capture our attention: our eyes immediately look for what is proportionately more dominant, brighter or shinier (it's proven that the famous "Donate Now" button on a web site in red is efficient).

In fundraising we know that any kind of campaign has a greater chance of response if:

a) It contains more images than words;

b) The images are of individuals (people or animals), possibly in the foreground;

c) These images are of children or puppies.

Fig. 3.29. Examples of use of faces in NSPCC, WWF, UNICEF and Smile Train.

For years, UNICEF in the Netherlands ran an annual fundraising campaign in which the face and the story of a single child was central to the overall campaign, which was themed on vaccination, nutrition, violence, etc. The face of this child was used online and offline in all communications, including direct mail, website, posters, press inserts, etc. These campaigns, with the use of a clear and recognizable image of an individual child, succeeded in recruiting 10,000—15,000 new supporters every year and raised millions of Euros.

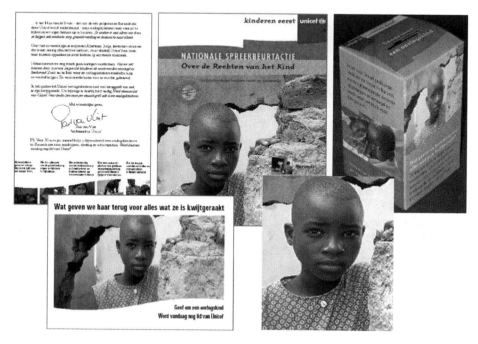

Fig. 3.30. UNICEF Netherlands Campaign.

Sound

Sound has a key role in activating our emotions and our decisions. According to neuroscientist and music producer Daniel J. Levitin, the auditory system is more rapidly activated when there is an unexpected event.[41] Think of a sudden sound that makes us jump, turn our head, or cover our ears. The auditory system—and then the sounds we perceive—is the system that's faster and more important in alerting us to danger. The most fascinating thing Levitin has found, however, is that when we listen to music, our brain activates in various other areas, including those involved in reward and pleasure and, at the same time, areas involved in movement.

---

41. Levitin, Daniel J. *This is Your Brain on Music: Understanding a Human Obsession*, Atlantic Books, 2008.

In fact, have you ever thought why some tunes make us tap our feet or hands? Music also activates the mesolimbic system (see Chapter 1), which is the system that releases chemicals that make us feel energized or releases a hormone with opiates (dopamine) that makes us feel good and functions as a reward mechanism.

Dan Hill, who measured the emotional response to some radio spots, provides us with examples of how the sounds (tone of voice) generate various types of responses:

a) People are about 24 percent more excited when listening to commercials with higher volume;

b) A voice with a low tone works best because it is associated with competence and authority;

c) Research indicates that those who speak more quickly have more influence on the listening audience;

d) The pause: 10 percent of all the emotional responses to advertising messages occur during pauses, as they serve to reinforce curiosity and the element of surprise.

In the two examples presented earlier, Fiona and Rachel, music plays a key role in activating the emotions. In the case of Fiona, the Avril Lavigne song, "I am with you," perfectly accompanies the video through rhythm, but also through the lyrics that seem to describe the situation experienced by Fiona. In the case of Rachel, the founder of charity: water, Scott Harrison, recalls that when he decided to produce this video he already had in mind the song that would accompany it, which is "Resolve" by Sleeping At Last, a group that produced sound tracks for shows like *Twilight* and *Grey's Anatomy*.[42]

The ASPCA (the American animal protection organization), with its use starting in 2007 of the famous Sarah McLachlan song "Angel," raised as much as US$30 million through the donations of 200,000 new donors, the most successful fundraising campaign the ASPCA has ever had. The song was originally about the Smashing Pumpkins touring keyboard player Jonathan Melvoin, who overdosed on heroin and died in 1996. But it works perfectly for animal rescue. "Sarah made it possible to do in two minutes what took 30 minutes before," said Jo Sullivan, the organization's senior vice president for development and communications, referring to the long-form use of celebrities in the past. "She

---

42. http://www.youtube.com/watch?v=M3UB4YQrffU "Charity's video racks up more than a half a million views," http://www.prdaily.com/Main/Articles/13580.aspx

literally has changed the way we fund raise." Many of the roughly 200,000 new donors attracted to the organization through the advertisement were "annuity" donors who have pledged an average of $21 a month to the ASPCA.[43]

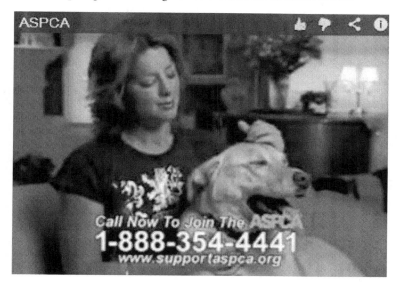

Fig. 3.31. ASPCA campaign with Sarah McLachlan.

In some successful fundraising TV spots, such as that of the UK RSPCA[44] on animal violence, the soundtrack is made up of animal noises (meows, barks, etc.). Dubbed by human voices, they seem to suggest and beg to viewers to help them.

Fig. 3.32. RSPCA DRTV.

---

43. "Ad Featuring singer proves bonanza for A.S.P.C.A", New York Times, December 5, 2008. http://www.nytimes.com/2008/12/26/us/26charity.html?em&_r=0
44. RSPCA Campaigns – Voices, http://www.youtube.com/watch?v=dsnOxmp7zbM

When we use social media and the web in particular, we should use sensory stimuli such as music, words and videos from the protagonists and beneficiaries of our organizations. For example, in UNICEF's AIDS campaign that I developed in 2005 (www.timetodrawtheline.com) visitors are greeted by an aid field worker who moves and talks introducing the campaign.

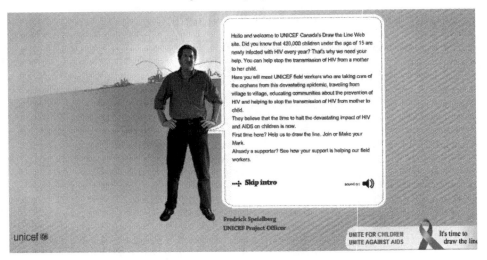

Fig. 3.33. UNICEF campaign on children and HIV AIDS.

Odours and scents

Should fundraising also have a particular smell? Surely scent has a very strong impact in the activation of emotions because perfumes and smells come straight and unmediated to the limbic and mesolimbic system—the emotional part of the brain.

Some experiments, for example, have found that our mood improves significantly when we smell a pleasant fragrance, and other studies have found that consumers are willing to spend more for a product located on a shelf or in a scented shop area, rather than in areas without any fragrance.

"75 percent of the emotions we generate on a daily basis are affected by smell. Next to sight, it is the most important sense we have," said Martin Lindstrom, author of *Brand Sense: How to Build Powerful Brands Through Touch, Taste, Smell, Sight and Sound.*[45]

Many advertisers are now seeing that happier customers and those who remember your brand and linger longer are the ones that can associate a product

45. Lindstrom, Martin. *Brand Sense: Building Powerful Brands Through Touch, Taste, Smell, Sight & Sound,* 2010.

or brand with a smell. Academic and industry research reveals that incorporating scent has a profound impact on how consumers regard a brand. The right ambient scenting solution can subtly prompt consumers to spend more time in retail environments and can be an effective means of drawing people into your store

Diffusing the right aroma can reinforce your brand identity, create the perfect ambiance for your clients, employees and guests, and differentiate your business from your competitors.

In a New Balance shoe store in Beijing, a consulting firm introduced Chinese shoppers to the U.S. brand through a sensory store experience. A nostalgic wood and leather scent was used to convey the heritage and craftsmanship of the brand. Shoppers spent twice as much money compared to similarly sized stores elsewhere, as the atmosphere induced them to linger.

In a study conducted by the University of Southern Brittany, the researchers found that a good fragrance can stimulate philanthropy. In an experiment, they dropped some items such as gloves or handkerchiefs outside a bakery and outside a clothing store and saw that many more people returned the lost items to the bakery than to the clothing store.[46] Could the smell of fresh bread further entice your donors?

James Hammond, a British fundraising consultant,[47] argues that the non-profit and fundraising sectors have not fully exploited the power of odours and scents. For example, he asks, who has smelled our organization? How can we recreate the perfume or the smell of the reasons why we work? Is it possible to describe the smell of poverty or recreate the smell of a forest that is about to disappear?

Objects and tactility

Despite the strong relationship between emotions and multisensory experience, many fundraising techniques and strategies still rely primarily on words (written or spoken) and only partly on the images. Fundraisers do not yet fully understand how to use other senses like smell or tactility. On the contrary, the touch of something has a deep connection with the activation of emotions and the formation of memories.

In a study conducted by V.S. Ramachandran and David Brang of the University of California,[48] the two scientists found that when we touch something,

---

46. "The power of freshly baked bread to stimulate altruism," November 18, 2012. http://www.fundraising.co.uk/blog/2012/11/18/power-freshly-baked-bread-stimulate-altruism

47. "Why fundraising needs to comes to its senses," http://www.brandhalo.co.uk/pdf/FundraisingArticle1.pdf

48. "Tactile-emotion synaesthesia," December 1, 2008. http://scienceblogs.com/neurophilosophy/2008/12/01/tactile-emotion-synaesthesia/

we activate a "synesthesia,"—a connection between two apparently separated areas of the brain: one regulating the tactile part or movements, and the limbic system that regulates emotions and memory. For example, some experiment participants revealed that a multicoloured toothpaste made them feel anxious, candle wax made them feel embarrassed or a smooth metal made them feel calm and quiet.

The effectiveness of objects and enabling "touch" in fundraising campaigns is well known and is connected with the idea of providing donors with a tangible element when we make the ask. Oral rehydration sachets (ORS, for rehydrating children), used by UNICEF, or bracelets for measuring malnutrition levels, used by UNICEF and MSF, have been at the core of successful fundraising campaigns for many years, both by direct mail and in face-to-face meetings.

 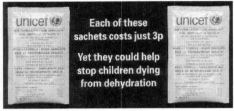

Fig. 3.34. ORS sachet from UNICEF and malnutrition bracelet from MSF.

Another example of a campaign that recorded excellent results in terms of responses and donations is the pen used by Amnesty International in its direct mail. The pen was in the letter with the message that what you have in your hand is an instrument of torture, but it can be an instrument of change.

Fig. 3.35. Appeal from Amnesty International.

In my experience, even in dialogue with a CEO or a major donor, the tangibility of objects helps in exemplifying your case. Objects evoke emotions, often a key element in influencing and persuading the donor. In meetings with potential donors, I always brought a bag of items that exemplify tangibly UNICEF's work: the ORS sachets; the bracelet that measures malnutrition; a notebook and a pen to exemplify education; and an empty syringe that is used for vaccination against polio. These objects have the power to create for the donor a story and an emotion that connects them with the stories and emotions created by our words and images.

Words

Although the focus of our brain is mainly on images, words constitute a decisive role in activating our emotions.

Words, heard or read, especially metaphors and adjectives, can activate the emotional part of the brain and get someone to donate or to support a cause.

First, the words may serve to create or evoke other sensory emotions like smell, taste or tactile experience.

In a 2006 study published in the Journal *NeuroImage*, researchers in Spain asked participants to read words connoted with strong odours, along with neutral words.[49] They observed through MRI what was happening in the brains of those who participated. When participants read the Spanish words for "fragrance" and "coffee," their primary olfactory cortex lit up; when they read words meaning "chair" and "key," the same area remained inactive.

The way the brain responds to metaphors has received particular attention from neuroscientists and marketers. A research team at Emory University observed that when we read a metaphor, the same sensory cortex responsible for perception through touch is activated. Metaphors like, "The singer had a velvet voice" or "Butterfingers" awaken the sensory cortex; it does not activate with similar phrases, such as, "The singer had a pleasant voice," or "He had weak hands."

Adjectives work in stimulating and activating emotions. In a study, Brian Wansink of Illinois University[50] created an experiment to see the effect of creating a restaurant menu with food descriptions loaded with emotional significance—specifically, geographical or nostalgic adjectives. For example, "Luscious Italian fillet of fresh fish" vs. "Fillet of fresh fish"; "Tender grilled chicken fillet" vs. "Fillet

---

49. "Your Brain on Fiction," *The New York Times*, March 12, 2012 http://www.nytimes.com/2012/03/18/opinion/sunday/the-neuroscience-of-your-brain-on-fiction.html?pagewanted=all&_r=0
50. Wansink, Brian; Koert van Ittersum and James E. Painter. "How descriptive food names bias sensory perceptions in restaurants," *Food Quality and Preference* 16 (2005), pages 393–400.

of grilled chicken"; "Velvety chocolate pudding" vs. "Chocolate and zucchini pudding using Great-Grandmother's recipe." The menu using sensory adjectives helped to sell 27 percent more than the neutral menu with bland descriptions. Not only that, customers were also much more satisfied at the end of meals whose menu was full of adjectives.

Adjectives act on an unconscious level (not involving the rational part) and contribute to the decision to order or buy a certain product. Roger Dooley proposed a typology of adjectives helping to activate the emotions and, in turn, somehow influence our decisions:

a) Vivid adjectives. "Freshly caught" is more effective than "fresh"; "sharp pain" is less effective than an "unbearable pain."

b) Sensory adjectives. "Pizza baked in the wood-fired brick oven" or "Crispy fresh from the oven" are more effective than just "Pizza.". In the case of Fiona, the description of the condition in which they find her—"She urinated out of fear and just sat in it, frozen"—activates sensations and emotions of disgust.

c) Evocative and nostalgic adjectives. A cheese "aged in Vermont" evokes farms and pastoral landscapes, not Kraft factories. Think of the Barilla pasta ads in the 1980s, which focused on a pasta that means family, the warmth of home when it's raining outside, etc.

d) Specific adjectives. "Wild Alaskan salmon" immediately recalls the image of a healthy fish swimming free in pristine rivers.

Words can function as well as images but only if, points out Roger Dooley, they tell a story. In the case of the successful Google ads mentioned early in this section, words are telling a story and therefore it works. The same happens in the case of the famous "Girl Effect," sponsored by Nike to support women's rights; it has been seen by over 3 million people (http://www.youtube.com/watch?v=WIvmE4_KMNw). It uses only a succession of words and graphic illustrations, but tells a story.

Nobody knows the power of words for fundraising like Mal Warwick,[51] the guru of direct mail for non-profit. According to Warwick these are some of the cardinal rules for the use of the words in direct mail:

---

51. Warwick, Mal. *How to Write Successful Fundraising Letters*, The Jossey-Bass Nonprofit Guidebook Series, 2008.

a) Always use "I" and, most often, "you." We must remember that we write as an individual writing to another individual and not an organization writing to a generic donor. The repeated use of "You" gives importance to the other person we are writing and helps establish a relationship. The formal use of Mr. or Sir or Madame are not advisable because they create distance with a potential donor.

b) Ask for money, not support. The request for financial aid is the primary reason for the letter. We need to ask for it in a clear and explicit way, and repeatedly state why we need their money.

c) Do not think only about the letter but the whole package. We must always think that there is not only the letter but also an envelope and the attachments (such as a brochure, a payment slip, etc.), and we must be sure that all these elements have consistency in terms of phrases used. Using phrases and emotional images in the response mechanism (such as bulletins) can increase response.

d) Use simple language. Avoid numbers and statistics, acronyms and abbreviations or foreign words. Repeat important words often, and highlight them with underlines and bold text.

e) Use a simple format. Text should be easy and simple to read. A person reads a piece of mail in this sequence: before the P. S.; the signatory; the subject; and, only after reading these elements, they will read the text of the letter.

ADVICE AND PRACTICAL TOOLS

The emotions and decisions are multi-sensory based. If we want to convince someone to donate or support our cause, we have to use the full spectrum of the senses: images, sounds, smells, objects and words.

The images are the most important part of any communication because two-thirds of the stimuli that reach the brain are visual and 50 percent of our brain is dedicated to managing visual stimuli. Using dynamic images, preferably the face of individuals and, if possible, of children or puppies, has a greater impact than other visual elements.

Sounds are essential in activating the emotional part of the brain. Music in particular acts on the mesolimbic system that releases chemicals such as dopamine or oxytocin and creates feelings of well-being. Finding the right music or sounds to express the emotions of your campaign is crucial to convince and mobilize donors and supporters.

Scents and smells, though often underestimated, are among the most powerful activators of emotions as they arrive to the sensory part of the brain in a non-mediated way, activating both emotions and memories.

Objects and the tactile part of an appeal constitute a very important element to activate emotions and decisions. Use objects that illustrate the cause for which we are concerned, or the work of our organization helps enormously to anchor an emotion to a deeper feeling in our brains.

Finally, words, even if they appeal to the conscious and rational part of the brain, can have great power in the mobilization and activation of emotions. Words with a strong sensorial connotation, adjectives and metaphors have a great capacity to excite donors.

For better or for worse: The power of positive and negative emotions

Is there a specific formula for the optimal use of emotions? Which emotions work best in fundraising?

Emotions exist in a range and along a spectrum, with various degrees of intensity, and there is no one emotion that is more powerful than another. In addition, emotions are never experienced in isolation but in real life, and are always experienced in active combination with each other, resulting in myriad mental states and emotional nuances.

However, most of the key emotions are negative. According to Dan Hill and other researchers, this is due to the evolution of our brain: We are programmed to be more careful and are better equipped to respond to negative emotions. To survive, we must use our senses to perceive dangers and understand what we must do: flight or fight, defend or attack?

Also, in advertising, the use of negative emotions generates more attention and involvement than positive emotions. In market research by Millward Brown,[52] researchers analyzed the level of involvement generated by 60 different types of ads, and found out that ads using mainly negative emotions can create greater involvement among consumers.

CORRELATIONS BETWEEN EMOTION AND ENGAGEMENT		
Millward Brown engagement scale	Ameritest flow of emotion	
Base: N = 60 ads	Positive emotion correlations	Negative emotion correlations
Active positive		
Interesting	-0.02	+0.31
Involving	-0.18	+0.32
Unique	-0.20	+0.44
Active negative		
Irritating	-0.20	+0.40
Unpleasant	-0.16	+0.45
Disturbing	-0.14	+0.43
Passive positive		
Soothing	0.29	-0.40
Mellow	0.23	-0.42
Nice	0.10	-0.44
Passive negative		
Ordinary	-0.12	-0.19
Weak	-0.05	0.20
Boring	-0.04	0.00
Overall engagement	-0.19	+0.49

Fig. 3.36. Power of negative emotions.

52. Young, Chuck. "The use of negative emotions in advertising," World Advertising Research Center 2006. http://www.ameritest.net/images/upload/The percent20Use percent20of percent20Negative percent20Emotions.pdf

In the following table you can see how the level of consumer engagement is measured. In a frame-by-frame comparison between emotions and the level of attention and involvement generated by two ad spots, the one that uses mostly negative emotions generates more attention.

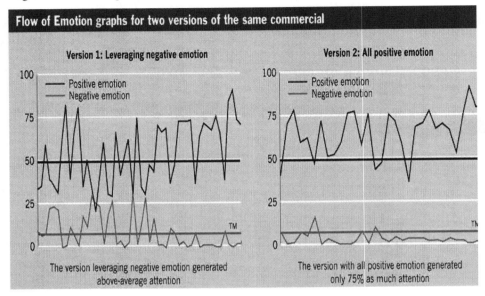

Fig. 3.37. Power of negative emotions in two ad spots.

Adrian Sergeant[53] recalls that the use of negative emotions leads to a better level of response also in fundraising. Analyzing the campaigns of WSPA (World Society for the Protection of Animals, today WAP), Bagozzi and Moore saw that the commercials that use negative emotions like sadness produce greater empathy among donors. Vitaglione and Burnett have seen that in campaigns on victims of accidents caused by drunk drivers, evoking emotions like anger generates a greater level of empathy among viewers—what they call "empathic anger"—resulting also in higher level of donations.[54]

However, when a negative emotion is activated, we feel at the same time the need or the desire for a positive finale and this can also activate changes in behaviour. Donating to an organization, according to Sergeant, is a way to overcome negative emotions. Positive emotions generated though the possibility of donating allow us to "imagine how the same story could end in a positive way."

53. Merchant A.; Ford J.B; and Sargeant, A: "Charitable Organizations' Storytelling Influence on Donors' Emotions and Intentions," *Journal of Business Research*, 63 (2010), pages 754-762.

54. Richard P. Bagozzi and David J. Moore, "Public Service Advertisements: Emotions and Empathy Guide Prosocial Behavior," *Journal of Marketing*, Vol. 58, No. 1, Jan. 1994, pages 56-70

Various studies have shown that sadness, for example, motivates us to give, and sad individuals are more inclined to donate to an organization if they believe that the act of giving will make them feel better. Indeed, we have already seen in the previous chapter that when we give, the brain releases substances that make us feel better (such as dopamine and oxytocin).[55]

In an experiment conducted by Sergeant,[56] a group of donors received two distinct messages: one containing the problem through the story of two children who have never been to school (evoking negative emotions), and another with a message including the possibility to donate to an organization that buys books, chairs and desks for educational programs (thus communicating positive emotions).

The researchers saw that the two emotions (negative and positive) play a complementary role in motivating people to donate, and even determine the ability to donate. Those with a positive outcome worked better also in terms of the value of donations received.

Fig. 3.38. Positive and negative emotions in two SOS Village mailings.

55. Manucia, Gloria K.; Donald j. Baumann and Cialdini, Robert B. "Mood influences on helping: Direct effects or side effects? ," *Journal of Personality and Social Psychology*, Vol 46(2), Feb. 1984, pages 357-364.
56. Merchant, A.; J. B. Ford; et al.: "Charitable Organizations' Storytelling Influence on Donors' Emotions and Intentions," *Journal of Business Research*, 63(7): 754-7622010.

The winning formula—"negative emotions + positive emotions = donations"—is indeed at the heart of many successful campaigns.

One of the best examples is Comic Relief, a campaign in England launched 30 years ago (http://www.comicrelief.com). This 1985 campaign, which includes a BBC TV program invented by Richard Curtis (director of films like *Four Weddings and a Funeral*, *Bridget Jones's Diary* and *Notting Hill*) and comedians, has raised to date 750 million pounds (890 million euros). The winning formula of Comic Relief—which, after a month of widespread mobilization and fundraising finishes with a prime-time show on BBC—is to alternate reportages and very touching emotional films with comedy sketches or comic adaptations of famous British TV shows such as *Doctor Who*, *Mr. Bean*, *Masterchef*, etc. In this way the viewer is taken on a roller coaster ride of emotions, because if there's too much sadness viewers would be overwhelmed and turn it off; and if there's too much comedy, no money would be raised. Moreover, the comedy acts as a punctuation, a kind of break from the heart-wrenching video from the field.

ADVICE AND PRACTICAL TOOLS

There is no established formula that guarantees any particular message or image will trigger the right emotions. It is also very hard to clearly indicate which emotions works better for fundraising. In general, our brains are hard wired, in evolutionary terms, to respond better to negative stimuli and emotions (sadness, fear, anger) than positive ones.

Surely, a good use of images and stories that have the ability to turn negative emotions into positive ones will have a high level of attention and participation and will be successful in fundraising. The chance to donate and contribute to a cause can be a powerful stimulus that activates positive emotions, which in turn help make a donor feel happy and satisfied by overcoming the negative feelings that may not necessarily lead to an action.

Chapter 4

Ethics and Morals:
When and how is using emotions
for fundraising right?

The use of emotional marketing and fundraising, especially through provocation and strong images, has been criticized on many occasions and in different contexts. In the U.K. and other countries, the debate has raged for many years with mixed results. Journalists, government and some nonprofit organizations often set limits on the use of certain video and images believed to be too emotional.

In the excellent summary by Dan Dufuor[57] from The Good Agency, the discussion in the U.K. is an old one and very articulated. Some TV ad spots and campaigns have been withdrawn or blocked by the advertising watchdog, such as that by Barnardo's that used images of children with cockroaches in their mouth or syringes in their arms with the message, "There are no silver spoon for children born into poverty." Even some images, such as those used by organizations like Operation Smile showing before and after an operation on children with cleft lips and palates were rejected or censored by media or watchdogs.

The new phrase describing the critical use of certain emotions in fundraising is "pornography of poverty" or development pornography. According to the authors, this term refers to any type of media, in writing, photography or movie, that exploits the conditions of the poor in order to generate sympathy in the audience to increase donations or support for a given cause. The pornography of poverty is typically associated with black people, usually poor Africans and children, with pictures or descriptions of people who are malnourished or powerless. The stereotype of the pornography of poverty is, according to the authors, the African child with a swollen belly, staring at the camera, waiting to be rescued.

Some nonprofit organizations have been advocating for the abolition of negative images or those evoking negative emotions such as anger or sadness.

---

57. "Do you need to be 'negative' to fundraise?" November 12, 2012. http://www.thegoodagency.co.uk/negative-fundraise/

Some years ago, for example, Oxfam launched a controversial campaign that, instead of showing African children suffering, leveraged more the natural beauty of that continent.[58] Other large international organizations have issued internal guidelines to prohibit the use of negative images in their own communication.

Let's try to understand the critical issues on the use of emotions in communication and fundraising, without claiming to have the final world on a debate that is very articulated. I am constantly discussing animatedly with communications colleagues, fundraisers, managers, board members, journalists and even the so-called "beneficiaries" about this issue.

The main subjects of this debate can be summarized as follows: the protection of the dignity of the beneficiaries; the reinforcement of stereotypes; the manipulation of the donor; and the emotional costs.

Does tapping into emotions violate the dignity of the beneficiaries?

One of the points often invoked by critics of the so-called "pornography of poverty" in fundraising is that images and descriptions of poverty often affect the rights and dignity of the people who are supposed to be helped; that using child images (or images of other vulnerable persons, such as women, animals, the elderly, sick, disabled, homeless, etc.) is violating their dignity by showing them only in a negative light. It is a sensitive issue because actually there is a risk of abuse of stereotypical images if there's no protection of those involved.

While on one hand there is definitely a tendency to use the same cliché images in fundraising, it is also true that the use of these images or words is based on solid experience and a rigorous practice (based on thousands of tests), which has shown that they work better in fundraising compared to neutral or happy images. Neuroscience, as we have seen, often confirms the practical knowledge of fundraising:

- For evolutionary reasons our brain responds more to negative emotions (although, as repeatedly stressed, positive emotions generated by the act of giving or showing the solution are just as important);
- The vast majority of the stimuli that manages our brains are visual and, between these stimuli, images of human faces generate more attention and empathy.

While we can discuss how to use emotions in communication in general (but

---

58. "Africa image harming aid effort, says charity Oxfam," BBC, December 26, 2012. http://www.bbc.co.uk/news/uk-20842827?ocid=socialflow_twitter_africa

no one seems to debate so critically on the use of the emotions or strong images in commercials for Volkswagen, Coca Cola or Barilla), when it comes to raising funds, the main objectives of the communication are:

a) Draw attention to difficult problems and their causes, in a world with limited attention in which every minute 200 million emails are sent, 600,000 Facebook messages are posted and each one of us watch 50 commercials per day;

b) Create an emotional connection with the audience, convince and inspire them to give their money to an idea, a project, a vision of the world.

Derek Humphries,[59] a TV expert for nonprofits, claims: "The problem with too much fundraising is that it is not shocking enough. Sometimes this is because issues become sanitized by charity communicators. And sometimes it's because agencies and/or clients become too concerned with being overtly creative. Important causes can end up looking like they might win a creative award rather than inspire a response. Such work can look expensive, often even when it isn't. And because too many fundraisers and their agencies dress up ugly issues in creative glad rags, too many compelling causes become fictionalized. I'd argue we should be doing the opposite. As fundraisers and campaigners we have a duty to tell the truth and to reveal the need so that people have the opportunity to help. If we obscure the need, then we deny people the chance to help. Which is pretty daft when there are so many wrongs in the world that need righting."

And it is difficult not to use negative emotions or communicate only positive images when we are dealing with a world where there are:

- 1 billion malnourished people.
- 250 million victims of war.
- 300 million victims of natural disasters.
- 2.5 billion people without clean water and latrines.
- 45 million refugees and displaced persons.
- 35 million people with AIDS.
- 1.3 billion people living on less than two Euros per day.

From a technical point of view, it is possible to preserve the dignity of beneficiaries using actors in the reconstruction of stories and critical situations or problems, or using other creative solutions like in the case of the TV spot by the organization NSPCC in UK who deals with domestic violence on children. The

---

59. "It's shocking: How we use imagery in fundraising."August 10, 2012. http://www.fundraising.co.uk/blog/2012/08/10/it% 80 %99s-shocking-how-we-use-imagery-fundraising

campaign used cartoon characters instead of children to explain what happens to a child when it is subject to violence.

Fig. 4.39. NSPCSC DRTV using cartoon characters.

Do emotions reinforce stereotypes?

The second criticism of the use of emotional elements in fundraising is that it helps reinforce the stereotypes and perceptions about the problem or causes that you want to remove. For example, African children starving, looking emaciated, abandoned and homeless, and those suffering from certain diseases or disabilities. For example, to combat stereotypes, the Oxfam campaign referenced above wanted to change the perception of Africa, and instead of spreading images of hunger or poverty uses images on landscapes, or the economy, with slogans such as, "Let's make Africa famous for its epic landscapes, not hunger." However, this can be good for awareness and changing perceptions, but not fundraising. Who will give to a tourist ad?

Fig. 4.40. OXFAM campaign.

The emergence of numerous non-profit organizations and similar campaigns, or at least campaigns on similar problems (poverty, malnutrition, AIDS, etc.) over the past 30 years, contributed to the use of similar images, in particular those relating to Africa. However, many fundraising campaigns do not reach their goal because they use too-sophisticated images, their messages are too complex and they fail to create an emotional connection with the audience, only raising limited funds.

I believe that we must distinguish between the different objectives of fundraising, communication, awareness and advocacy. In fact, I think there is a fundamental part of the non-profit communication that has to do with challenging preconceptions, stereotypes and prejudices, and is aimed at changing opinions and protecting the rights of the most vulnerable from abused imagery. But there is also an equally important part that is fundraising, and this has to do with creating an emotional connection with donors through the needs or the problems we are dealing with—often through crude words and/or shocking images if and when needed—and create hope through the opportunity to donate. Think about it: How can we convince donors of the need of donate for Syria, a devastating war going on for years? We need stories and emotions, and possibly crude and shocking words and pictures. Otherwise, Syria will go unnoticed in the sea of fundraising appeals.

Instead of criticizing words or pictures in fundraising campaigns, we should be clear that there are different functions and objectives of communication: some need to fight stereotypes, change opinions and convince the public, and others need to excite and convince the public to financially support our cause and organization. Thus, the campaign of Oxfam on Africa can easily exist with other fundraising campaigns that use different logic, methods, images and words.

Does using emotions manipulate donors?

One of the most frequent accusations is that fundraising is, when it comes down to it, pure commercial marketing. Some say that, ethically and morally, fundraising techniques manipulate, and create an illusion that serves only to confuse and misuse the good faith of donors to subtly twist their arms into making a donation that they actually do not want to make. This simplistic and distorted vision of emotions maintains that fundraising is manipulating the public and generating a sense of guilt to lead them to believe that without their donation someone will suffer or die.

As Jeff Brooks said,[60]

> "…we are integrated systems. There's not a rational side that's separate from the emotional, subconscious, hormonal parts of us. Appealing to one while bypassing the others is not possible.
>
> If you think you're going to be 'non-manipulative' and only apply to the rational side of your audience, you'll still end up communicating on deep psychological levels. You'll just be doing an inept job of it. The subconscious emotional message you think you're omitting will still be there; it just won't be working with the rational messaging.
>
> While you're earnestly trying to persuade people to give, you'll be signaling something like:
>
> - You don't matter very much.
> - This problem is way too big for you to tackle.
> - This issue is not very important.
> - We're only pretending to like you.
> - You're way less educated than we are.
>
> And the unconscious part of your message will be much louder and more persuasive than the part you're so carefully focusing on.
>
> You can't make the unconscious part of your message go away. Something will fill those slots. Wouldn't you prefer to fill them with the message you want to send?
>
> Asking if unconscious communication is unfair is a meaningless question. The real questions are 'Am I doing it right?' and 'Am I telling the truth?'"

Brooks, who argues that it is not moral or ethical to use emotions in fundraising, makes two major errors:

1. *It still appeals to the emotions, but in the wrong way, using rationality.* Even if you try to build the message as flat, colourless and without any emotion, you still send donors an emotional message. But you generate an active rejection, boredom and disinterest so that in the end many people do not donate. That's bad fundraising.

---

60. http://www.futurefundraisingnow.com/future-fundraising/2012/01/all-fundraising-is-emotional-you-cant-leave-the-emotions-out.html

2. *Use your own emotions, rather than the emotions of donors.* In this case, you may think that certain convictions (our emotions) are rational values (e.g . the sense of injustice for certain situations) that are automatically transferable to donors. Besides being arrogant, this attitude also leads to very ineffective fundraising.

The discoveries of neuroscience and their applications cannot be classified as ethical or not. Emotions are not a tactic or a gimmick; we cannot decide whether to turn them on or off. We cannot decide whether they are ineffective, if they disturb or annoy our audience, and therefore not to use them.

Emotionraising and its applications can only help us and help our organizations to be more effective—for example, by increasing the number of supporters and donations. Emotionraising is also a way to better respect what donors think or feel without trying to impose our messages or our values on them. Rather, we are trying to create an emotional connection with our cause.

How much will emotions cost?

One of the consequences (and criticisms) of emotional fundraising is that it has very high costs and requires investments. This is true, in part. Too many contemporary fundraising tools and media are outdated and limited. Direct mail, for example, can yield a good cost vs. income return, but not great income growth and volumes. In fact, data on responses to current direct mail is disappointing. Generally, prospect mass mailing responses are 0.1 percent - 0.5 percent of the total, and more than 50 percent of existing donors do not renew their donation via mailing.

When trying to understand the motivations of donors and the methods that work best, we are doing it with inadequate and outdated tools—for example, questionnaires and focus groups, that, as mentioned, reveal only part of the reason why people donate: the rational part.

The public and donors are more sophisticated than a simple letter or newsletter. Today through social media we are exposed to an incredible amount of stimuli—visual auditory, sensory, tactile, etc. The multi-sensory dimension of emotions suggests that fundraising communications and corresponding nonprofit communications should use more channels and multi-sensory content (video, TV, web), and invest in telling organizations' stories, dreams and successes in vivid and emotional manner, as Hollywood and the world of commercial advertising does.

Moreover, like commercial enterprises, non-profit organizations should invest more in research and techniques like those used by neuroscience and applied to the donation decision making process. Such techniques include eye tracking that measures where our visual attention is focused by analyzing the movement of the pupils; CT scan or MRI to identify which areas of the brain respond to our messages and images; analysis of micro-facial expressions; etc. These are all methods and techniques with a cost. However—and this is also a myth to dispel—neuro-marketing research on audience response to various campaigns and appeals can cost no more than $10,000-$15,000 US. This is because techniques are easy and cheap, laboratories are set up and, more important, the sample is small because emotional status is identifiable on a relatively small sample of donors and consumers.

The fact that the non-profit world cannot, in general, invest in techniques or spend on advertising—the consequences being ads that are cheap, look cheap and are ineffective—is one of the self-imposed limitations that Dan Pallotta identified in charities.[61] The current stereotype is that a nonprofit cannot afford to spend much money on fundraising activities because its money must be used for the cause itself, so it's unthinkable, even immoral, to use resources to produce and distribute a video, or to invest in costly research techniques.

The truth is that this is part of a moral paradigm that limits fundraising and the growth of non-profits. This paradigm wants charities and nonprofits to remain marginal and limited because they are not supposed to solve problems, only alleviate them. Where can we find the needed resources for many causes, such as the fight against cancer or the end of poverty? The idea that the nonprofit is primarily voluntary, charitable and based on generosity is often ridiculous. Just look, for example, at the advertising market. This amounted to about in $542 billion in 2016. How much of that was spent by nonprofits to raise the needed resources for hunger, famine, cancer, violence, etc.? It's negligible: less than 2 percent - 3 percent. One example cited by Pallotta shows that the American Society for Cancer Research spends on average $1 million a year on lobbying and advertising campaigns against smoking, while the tobacco industry spends over $9 billion on advertising. Who is going to win the war?

Emotional fundraising requires that nonprofits invest in creativity, in new media and in modern research techniques because, if you stay confined to current techniques and current assumptions and preconceptions, you are likely to be fighting in a world with inadequate and obsolete weapons compared those of marketing and commercial companies. And that's a world in which less than 1 percent of the public responds to your urgent appeals for funds.

---

61. Pallotta, Dan. *Charity Case: How the Nonprofit Community Can Stand Up For Itself and Really Change the World*, Jossey-Bass, 2012.

PART TWO

Emotions at work:
How to plan and implement
campaigns and strategies
that illuminate the mind,
warm hearts—and open wallets

"Genius is the ability to renew
one's emotions in daily experience."

—Paul Cezanne

INTRODUCTION

If emotions move the world (or at least guide our decisions and our actions), how do they activate empathy and sympathy towards our cause and our organizations, in particular pushing people to donate money, time and other resources?

Neuroscience, psychology, economics and marketing provide some scientific basis for understanding how and why emotions work, and in this second part of the book we will learn, through specific examples of fundraising successes and failures, how emotions work in practice.

In Chapter 5, we will return to six key emotions and find out how successful fundraising campaigns use emotions.

In Chapter 6, we will look at ten important techniques and methodologies for emotional fundraising, techniques that are based on the theories of experts like Robert Cialdini, Chip and Dan Heath, and Dan Hill.

Chapter 7 is devoted to understanding how emotions works for various types of donors, such as the general public, companies, foundations and major donors.

Chapter 8 will show how emotions are crucial, and often overlooked, in maintaining a lasting and fruitful relationship with our donors—not just in acquiring new ones.

Finally, in Chapter 9, we will see how emotions are crucial in the decisions and practice of will-making and legacies.

Chapter 5

Emotionraising:
How emotions convince,
seduce and influence
supporters and donors

Emotions get people to donate, and giving money activates reward mechanisms that make us feel better. If we cannot ignite emotions—make somebody angry, make them cry or smile, for or through our causes—we will hardly be able to move somebody to sign a petition, click on a Facebook page or, indeed, donate.

Emotionmeter©

JOY	AMAZEMENT	RAGE	LOATHING	GRIEF	TERROR
HAPPINESS	SURPRISE	ANGER	DISGUST	SADNESS	FEAR
Satisfaction	Curiosity	Annoyance	Boredom	Pensiveness	Worry

HIGH INTENSITY EMOTIONS/low intensity emotions
Adapted from Hill and Ekman

Fig. 5.41. States of emotional intensity, according to Ekman and The Emotionmeter©.

In the first part of this book, we saw how neuroscience helps us to understand some basic elements:

- Most of the emotions we feel are negative. Four out of six key emotions are negative (anger, sadness, disgust and fear); one is neutral (surprise); and one is positive (happiness).
- Negative emotions generate more attention and audience involvement than other emotions. In two campaigns that use positive and negative emotions, the latter always gets better results in terms of response and donations; however, use of only negative emotions will not necessarily lead to the act of donating if there is not a positive solution (also imagined) to the negative emotions.
- The chance to contribute to solving a problem via a donation generates a positive emotion—happiness—that's activated by substances such as oxytocin and dopamine released into the blood from the brain.
  ° Emotions are not to be confused with feelings, which are emotions that make it into our consciousness. Emotions are measurable through a variety of instruments like EEG, MRI, etc., which show what happens when we watch a video, listen to a story, etc. Feelings are what people experience sometime after this experience. Feelings are what remains of emotions and are recorded in our memory so that when we recreate the same experience, emotions unfold once again.
- Emotions are also the basis of memory formation through the amygdala. So, when we activate a strong enough emotion through our messages, we can set in motion memory storage mechanisms, which means that we can re-use the emotions that were ignited initially, reactivating the same actions and behaviours, such as a new donation or a legacy.
- Emotions are not generated in isolation, but are always situated along a spectrum of intensity and in combination with some other emotion (emotions can be at high and low intensity, and emotions in real life are combined, resulting in other states like embarrassment, guilt, melancholia, etc.).
- On the other side of emotions, according to Dan Hill, are the states of mind that are less intense as they are not associated with a sensory stimulus, but endure as long-term emotions.

We have seen how the six key emotions work and how in reality they push people to donate to causes and fundraising appeals. Let's look at how each of them can play a role in fundraising.

Negative emotions

Negative emotions have a greater force than other emotions in attracting our attention, in engaging our senses and in activating mechanisms of empathy or rejection. According to neuroscientists, this has an evolutionary explanation because our attention was originally supposed to be constantly on alert in order to react quickly to hazards and other negative situations.

Fundraisers know that the use of words and images that evoke emotions such as fear and sadness can, if used properly, produce good responses in terms of donations and donors. Since we also know that the stories are the most powerful communication tool to activate emotions, we know that for stories to be interesting they must contain at least one emotion such as sadness, fear or anger.

Jonathan Gottschall said that hell is often a good subject for stories: "The stories always relate to someone who has a problem to solve." The protagonists strongly want something (to survive, conquer a woman or a man, regain a lost son, etc.). However, they face major obstacles. Each story, whether comic, tragic or romantic, concerns the efforts of someone who desperately wants something and obstacles (including the risk of death) are the main part of this story. Obstacles and challenges make you appreciate a happy ending as a positive outcome. Successful fundraising is often a story of protagonists who face great obstacles to get what they want. Like in the movie *The Godfather* or the opera *La Traviata*, donors are so involved in our stories because they know that their small contribution can help the protagonist (a woman or a child, a village or a museum, a university or a hospital) to achieve his/her purpose and to resolve, at least in part, his/her problems.

Rationally we do not like to think that we respond to emotions such as fear or anger, but emotionally our brain is more inclined to react to this type of input rather than to rational or positive stimuli.

- In a study of about 5,000 fundraising spots for a public TV channel in the United States, most of the donations came as a response to emotions such as fear or sadness (evoked by the idea that the TV channel could close for lack of funds).
- Appeals and fundraising campaigns that use sad images r nations than those using faces with happy or neutral ex

62. D. Smal
of Marketing Re

Mean donations by emotion expression in study 1

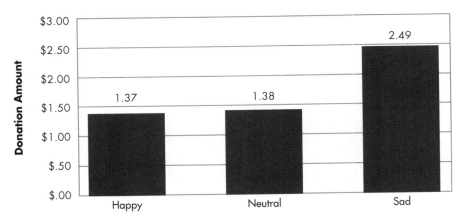

Fig. 5.42. Power of negative emotions in an experiment by Small and Verocchi.[62]

Fear

Fear is a powerful emotion. It can create a connection with donors by stimulating empathy toward someone who is experiencing a dangerous situation: a refugee on the run, an animal or a child fleeing violence, a monument that is collapsing. Fear can also work by recreating situations for a potential risk that might also affect a donor (as, for example, in the case of diseases such as cancer, AIDS, etc.).

Fig. 5.43. Use of fear of violence in DRTV spot by NSPCC and RSPCA.

Fear is one of the oldest and most powerful emotions and is deeply rooted in our brains from an evolutionary point of view. This is because fear helps us to ˙˙ id risks and dangers. The amygdala function, in fact, is almost exclusively a

N. Verocchi: "The Face of Need: Facial Emotion. Expression on Charity Advertisements," *Journal* ˙rch*, Vol. XLVI (December 777 2009).

fear management mechanism. Fear is so powerful it can trigger responses in our body like muscle paralysis, increased heart rate and hyperventilation or sweating. The writer Karen Thompson Walker said, "Our fears are an extraordinary gift of imagination, a way of seeing how the future could be when we are still in time to influence it. As with all great stories, fear helps us to focus on the next step, to assess carefully what will happen in the future."[63]

An example of the successful use of this emotion in fundraising is the campaign Obama for America (OFA), which helped raise funds for the re-election of Barack Obama. OFA raised over $690 million online only, mainly via email and SMS, from four million donors who donated an average of $53 each.

The key of the success of Obama's fundraising.[64] and the overall campaign, is the use of a large amount of data and much testing, especially through social media (Twitter, Facebook, email). One of the results of these tests was that in terms of content, the fundraising appeal that contained or evoked fear as predominant emotion (fear of losing the election, fear of not having the necessary funds to support the campaign against more wealthy opponents, etc.) worked far better despite criticism raised in the media.

Friend --

This week, we need to make some of the last, tough choices about what the final push of this grassroots organization will look like -- where we can compete and how fiercely.

It's a close race, and you hold the power here. According to our records associated with this exact email address:

- -- Your supporter ID is: ▓▓▓▓ ▓▓▓▓▓
- -- Most recent donation: $0
- -- Total amount donated in 2012: $0

It looks like you haven't given yet. That may be because you gave using a different email address than you're using now -- if we've got this wrong, I apologize.

But if you indeed have not yet given, there's still time. Just not very much -- this Friday is one of our last opportunities to plan for the final weeks of this campaign.

Fig. 5.44. An email used by the OFA campaign using fear.

---

63. Thompson Walker, Karen: "What fear can teach us," https://www.ted.com/talks/karen_thompson_walker_what_fear_can_teach_us/transcript

64. "TexMessage: Obama campaign is now using a new fundraising technique: guilt!" October 12, 2012 http://blog.chron.com/txpotomac/2012/10/texmessage-obama-campaign-is-now-using-a-new-fundraising-technique-guilt/

In this second example, addressed to so-called "lapsed" donors, OFA sent a summary of how much they had contributed so far, knowing from the data in their possession that they had not yet donated. The appeal suggests or evokes a sense of guilt among donors. "It looks like you haven't given yet. That may be because you gave using a different email address than you're using now; if we've got this wrong, I apologize. But if you indeed have not yet given, there's still time. Just not very much—this Friday is one of the last opportunities…"

> Friend --
>
> Whatever happens at the vice presidential debate tonight, we need to respond quickly and forcefully.
>
> With 26 days to go, we can't just sit and wait for someone else to set the record straight. That's how elections are lost.
>
> We won last time because people like you stepped up and chipped in what they could to move the country forward. The stakes are even higher this time, so what are you waiting for?
>
> **Please make a donation of $5 or more right now to see this campaign through the finish line.**

Fig. 5.45. An email used by the OFA campaign using the guilt factor.

Fear is a powerful emotion that can engage the donor ("this is something that can happen to you" or "I can help save those who are in danger"). However, it also has its limits. As recalled by Dan Hill, fear used by itself, with no other emotion or without adequate call for action, can cause paralysis in the interlocutor (we do not know what will happen or we don't know what to do). And fear combined with sadness can leave us desperate or distressed—and also not knowing what to do.

Fear also works through the sense of guilt, which can be criticized from a moral or intellectual point of view, in spite of it working in fundraising. There are situations in which the two emotions (fear and sadness) overlap: it is sometimes difficult to identify which one is at work; are we afraid of feeling guilty, or we feel guilty because we are afraid? For example, commercials for detergents that use stains on the collar appeal both to fear (we try to avoid the embarrassment) and guilt, pushing someone to fix the problem before it occurs. In both situations, the detergent will prevent stains and solve the problem.

In the case of Obama, suggesting to supporters the scenario where there is an incumbent risk—the fundraising objective is not reached and they lose the election—may be applied, in a different manner, even to the non-profit world: "What will happen if we do not raise the money to help our beneficiaries, or to fight our enemy/disease? That is why we need your help and your support."

Sadness

Sadness has the power to ignite strong empathy and thus attract supporters and donations. On the one hand, as already explained, mirror neurons light up when we see situations that we recognize as painful (loss, lack, stress, etc.) and activate the same emotions (even physically) of those who suffer, while at the same time developing the need to search for a solution. Words and images (and also smells, tastes and objects) reactivate our memory—which we know is formed through emotions—and the sad, nostalgic or melancholic moods stimulate actions we once took to feel better.

In a fascinating book that is based on the latest findings in neuroscience, *Why Humans Like to Cry*, Michael Trimble[65] explains how tears, and crying in general as a result of an emotional state such as sadness, is a purely human characteristic. Animals do not cry when they are sad. The tears we shed when we cry watching a movie or listening to a particular melody are different (also chemically) from those we shed when our eyes are irritated or when we get hurt. The tears we shed when we are sad have a social communication function. Just think of the first thing a baby does when he/she is born: cries. On one hand we cry because we feel the same sadness and sorrow of those we observe (mirror neurons—seeing others suffering activates nerves and muscles around our eyes that provoke tears), and on the other hand we cry to communicate and share with others our sadness.

Marketing has studied the effects of sadness on the willingness to spend.[66] In an experiment, researchers have noted that sad people are likely to spend more. If psychology has already identified the phenomenon "misery is not miserly" or so-called "retail therapy," the experiment conducted by a group of researchers from Harvard, Carnegie Mellon, Stanford and Pittsburgh universities[67] has gone one step further, because it measured what happens to consumers when they shop after watching sad videos. One group of consumers watched a sad video of a person who talks about the death of a loved one, while a second group watched a generic video on coral reefs in Australia. The first group was willing to spend much more to buy products such as a simple bottle of water, spending up to 200 percent more

65. Michael Trimble, *Why Humans Like to Cry*. Tragedy, Evolution, and the Brain: The Evolutionary Origins of Tragedy, OUP Oxford, 2012
66. "Tragedy = Increased Spending," February 14, 2011 http://www.marketstar.com/blog/retail-channel/sadness-increased-spending/
67. Cynthia E. Cryder; Jennifer S. Lerner; James J. Gross; and Ronald E. Dah: "Misery Is Not Miserly. Sad and Self-Focused Individuals Spend More," *Psychological Science*, Volume 19—Number 6 200

than the actual price. What is interesting is that participants who went shopping after the videos were not aware of the state of mind stimulated by the earlier movies.

In fundraising, we know that sadness is a powerful weapon at our disposal, often abused or stereotyped in so-called "tearjerker" campaigns. Just think of the massive response in terms of donations after a natural disaster such as earthquakes, floods, famines. Or, as mentioned in the first part of this book, consider the mass response to little known causes that use extremely sad stories like that of Rachel used by charity: water.

In one example of a mailing for Sharp Hospice Care in the United States, Tom Ahern[68] explains how the emotional component of sadness played a key role in making this letter one that worked best for many years in terms of donations received. The mailing is addressed to occasional donors in order to make them become regular donors.

Dear Jane Doe,

This Memorial Day, you and I will share something special...

....a memory of what Sharp HospiceCare did for a person we hold dear.

In 1998, Peggy, my wife of 34 years, died of cancer.

Thanks to the people at Sharp HospiceCare, Peggy finished her days with dignity, free of suffering, at peace. Most important, she died at home in a circle of love, with her family and friends around her.

I don't need to tell you what Hospice means. You know.

But here's something you might not know: Hospice can't survive without your help. That's the plain, unvarnished truth. The kind of hospice care that you find at Sharp includes so many things that Medicare fees and other insurer reimbursements just won't pay for.

That's why I'm writing, to ask that you give a tax-deductible gift today – as much as you can afford – to help Sharp HospiceCare continue its mission.

Your gift goes immediately to work, helping other families cope successfully with the suffering, confusion, doubts and fears that surround a loved one's death.

Every gift is appreciated...and will do real good.

Your gift of $25 . . . helps purchase cleaning supplies for the volunteers who wash the windows and weed the gardens at Sharp's beautiful and serene new Lakeview Home.

Your gift of $250 . . . helps Sharp pay for chaplains specially trained in the difficult work of counseling grieving families.

Your gift of $500 . . . helps underwrite the cost of Sharp's amazing June retreat, a weekend of counseling and healing in the mountains . . . where two bewildered children who recently lost their mom can explore their feelings with other grieving kids, under the watchful eye of social workers . . . and begin to heal.

If you believe in Hospice as much as I do, please follow your heart and give with as much generosity as you can manage.

I hope you'll give at least $100 . . . for this special reason:

Gifts of $100 or more are "In memory of..." gifts.

When you give an "In memory of..." gift, both your name and the name of your loved one are featured and thanked in our annual donor report. (Of course, you can choose to remain anonymous if you prefer.)

I miss Peggy so much. I think of her all the time. I remember our wedding day, as if it were yesterday. You know, when you're saying your wedding vows and come to the end where you pledge "Until death do us part," you really don't think it will ever come true.

But it does. For all us, in some way. Loved ones die, and suddenly you don't know what to do.

That's when Sharp HospiceCare matters most. Please give today.

With my sincere thanks and appreciation this Memorial Day,

John X. Doe, MD (retired)

P.S. Each Memorial Day I do two things. I bring Peggy flowers, to tell her how much I still love her. And I give a gift to Sharp HospiceCare, in her name . . . because they cared for her when she needed them most, and now Sharp needs me.

Fig. 5.46. Example of mailing by Sharp HospiceCare.

68. http://www.sofii.org/node/518

The letter is dated Memorial Day, the day when Americans remember the people they care about the most, and it is written from a donor who speaks about his own experience at the hospice where his wife, Peggy, died. The letter's author, Tom Ahem, recalls keeping in mind emotional triggers such as sadness and anger, using phrases like the following:

"I miss Peggy so much. I think of her all the time. I remember our wedding day, as if it were yesterday. You know, when you're saying your wedding vows and come to the end where you pledge 'Until death do us apart,' you don't really think it will ever come true. But it does. For all of us, in some way. Loved ones die, and suddenly you don't know what to do."

"P.S. Each Memorial Day I do two things. I bring Peggy flowers, to tell her how much I still love her. And I give a gift to Sharp HospiceCare in her name…"

As in the case of fear, sadness in isolation can lead to people reacting slowly or may simply cause a block (we are so sad and we do not know what to do, other than be disappointed, have regret, and despair). Sadness can, however, activate virtuous behaviour—for example, through nostalgia, which works in the case of "donations in memory" or bequests. Nostalgia according to John Ford of Old Dominion University[69] has an important effect in stimulating the intention to donate.

Remember growing up with Kermit the Frog!
Kermit the Frog, Big Bird, Curious George … are some of the icons that generations of Americans have grown up with. Your donation to PBS can help us continue to provide wholesome entertainment.

 PBS

Relive the wonderful memories of the past!
Remember your university days … the learning, sports, friends, parties and graduation day … the fun and the dreams … those were the days!
Now, reconnect with the magic of the past by donating money to your University Alumni Association for a new football stadium for the students.

University Alumni Association

Fig. 5.47. Examples of use of nostalgia by PBS radio and a university.

69. Merchant, Altaf; Ford, John B.; Rose, Gregory: "How personal nostalgia influences giving to charity," *Journal of Business Research*, 2011, vol. 64, issue 6, pages 610-616.

Nostalgia plays a fundamental role in the case of bequests and wills, a very important source of funds for non-profit organizations. We will see in a separate chapter how emotions work in a legacy campaign.

Russell N. James, from Texas Tech University,[70] has tried to see with the help of MRIs what happens when you talk to donors about their willingness to leave a legacy to a non-profit organization. According to James, to name a nonprofit in a will, it is fundamental that the prospective donor sees the final chapter of his life as an autobiography. The fundraiser should find ways to emphasize the moments and events of how his organization was connected to donor's life and biography. For example, mention events, successes and images of the history of the nonprofit and connect them with those of the donor. Moreover, there is generally a natural tendency to avoid speaking of the will as it is closely related to death. Therefore, when an organization is able to involve the donor in a common nostalgic memory, showing what you did together or through the organization he/she supported, then the organization establishes a virtuous path leading to the decision to name the organization in the will.

Anger and disgust

As with other negative emotions (fear and sadness), anger and disgust can play a key role in convincing donors and supporters. Of the six key emotions, anger and disgust involve a quick decision and a very strong expectation for an instant result to relieve the feeling.

Anger more than any other emotion elicits active bodily reactions and evokes immediate action: think when about when we are angry and we kick a door, or bang a fist on the table, or even when we would like to hit someone or something.

Anger and indignation are very strong emotions that offer, if used properly, the possibility of involving donors and supporters to sign a petition or to make a gift. Some organizations, especially those concerned with human rights, use anger as their main emotion. Amnesty International and Greenpeace, for example, seek in all their campaigns to arouse anger and indignation among their supporters.

---

70. James, Russel N., "Cognitive skills in the charitable giving decisions of the elderly." *Educational Gerontology*, 37(7), 559-573 III.; (2011). James, R. N. III; Atiles, J. H.; & Robb, C. A: "Charitable giving and cognitive ability," *International Journal of Nonprofit and Voluntary Sector Marketing*, 16(1), 70-83.;. (2011).

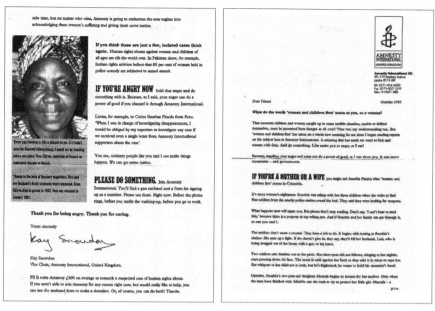

Fig. 5.48. Amnesty International use of anger.

This example, which is one of the most successful campaigns by Amnesty, makes explicit reference to anger. As the text says, "If you're angry now, hold that anger and do something with it. Because your anger can do a power of good if you channel it through Amnesty International."

War Child, a Dutch NGO that works to help the child victims of war, does so by explicitly calling on their donors to use anger.

Fig. 5.49. War Child.

Animal welfare organizations use anger as a predominant emotion by highlighting the conditions in which animals live or the violence to which they are subject.

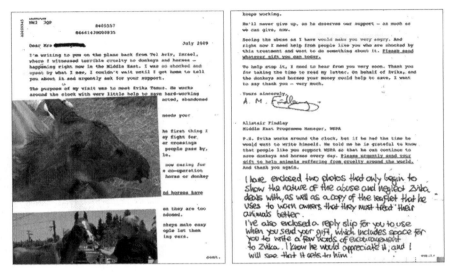

Fig. 5.50. WSPA mailing using anger.

In the case of this mailing from WSPA (World Society for Protection of Animals)—a mailing that had among the best results in terms of donations—a worker tells the story of the mistreatment of animals in Israel and even refers specifically to anger. "Seeing the abuse as I have would make you very angry. And right now I need help from people like you who are shocked by this treatment and want to do something about it."

Surprise

Surprise is a fundamental emotion to get the attention of potential donors and to activate other key emotions. Without surprise, few messages or campaigns will be remembered or noticed.

In a study on why certain fundraising campaigns become viral on social media,[71] a group of Australian and British scientists found that surprise, of all emotions, is essential to ensure that the message is widely spread. However, according to these researchers, surprise alone is not enough to trigger a specific action, such as donating or sharing, but should always be combined with other emotions.

---

71. Angela Dobele; Adam Lindgreen; Michael Beverland; Joëlle Vanhamme; Robert van Wijk: "Why pass on viral messages? Because they connect emotionally," *Business Horizons* (2007) 50, pages 291–304.

Emotions elicited in the different viral marketing campaigns						
Viral marketing campaign	Surprise	Joy	Sadness	Anger	Disgust	Fear
Weapons of Mass Destruction	✓		✓	✓		
Christmas Cards	✓	✓				
Raging Cow	✓		✓			
Honda Accord	✓	✓				
Motorola V70	✓	✓				
Red Cross	✓		✓			✓
Organization of Women's Freedom	✓				✓	
Save BNN	✓		✓	✓		
Rock the Vote	✓	✓				

Fig. 5.51. Surprise is the main emotion elicited in social media campaigns.

Astonishing listeners and donors is an essential element of any message that you want to have an impact. Communications gurus Dan and Chip Heath,[72] in their book *Made to Stick*, indicate surprise as one of the most important mechanisms to create memorable messages. According to the Heath brothers, ideas and unexpected messages or surprises are easier to remember because they make us think. However, surprise is a very ephemeral and quick emotion, and requires that you find an immediate answer to why you were surprised. We will return later in this book to how to incorporate elements that can surprise our donors. But suffice it to say that, clearly, if we want to motivate our audience we should use ingenuity to create big surprises wherever we can.

Greenpeace often uses surprise as a key emotion along with anger and fear. For example, in a highly successful campaign to stop the use of palm oil by multinationals, which causes deforestation of the natural habitat of the orang-utans in Borneo, Greenpeace used a video (http: // www.youtube.com / watch? feature = player embedded & v = VaJjPRwExO8) showing a bored clerk taking a break eating a KitKat, but instead of the traditional chocolate bar he is eating an Orangutan finger.

---

72. Chip and Dan Heath, *Made to Stick: Why Some Ideas Survive and Others Die*, Random House, 2007.

Fig. 5.52. Use of surprise by Greenpeace in a campaign against KitKat

This campaign has been a great success both in terms of audience (more than two million have seen it), and in terms of supporters taking action by posting thousands of messages to Nestle—resulting in the company deciding later to stop importing palm oil from Borneo.

Another very successful campaign that used surprise as the main emotion is the campaign created by Bono of U2 for Red to support, through the sale of specific products, the Global Fund to Fight AIDS, Tuberculosis and Malaria. The campaign, called "The Lazarus Effect," refers to the well-known story of Lazarus, who is called from the tomb by Jesus. This campaign features the stories and images of people living with AIDS before (a few weeks before death) and after (thanks to antiretroviral drugs), and explains how two pills a day you can bring an HIV patient back from death.

Fig. 5.53. The Lazarus Effect campaign.

The Lazarus Effect, promoted through Red products, has help raise more than $150 million for the Global Fund.

While surprise has great power to attract attention, if it is not used with an appropriate "call to action" it risks leaving a potential donor puzzled with a feeling of disorientation and disorder, because it is not clear what he/she should and can do. Many fundraising campaigns use surprise but are unable to transform this emotion into action that can channel the energy aroused.

Happiness

Happiness is perhaps the emotion most used by commercial marketing and advertising. Many campaigns and strategies such as those of Coca Cola and other famous brands use this emotion as their brand.

The examples are numerous: Nesquik has the slogan, "You can't buy happiness, but you can drink it." Dunkin' Donuts uses, "The happiest sandwich on Earth." And Nivea offers a body lotion to make you "Feel happy." Hugo Boss offers "Orange, the fragrance of happiness," and Clinique has a perfume called "Happy."

Through interactive campaigns, marketing has also tried to cultivate happiness. Coca-Cola launched the famous campaign "Open Happiness." This promotes the simple pleasures of life and encourages consumers to take a break to connect and share your happiness with others. In 2010 BMW developed the campaign "Stories of Happiness" with video content that highlight the joy of driving. Yahoo launched the "Purple Kindness Acts" campaign, the purpose of which is to spread happiness and encourage small acts of kindness.

All these campaigns use and are inspired by the "feel good factor"—generally, that if a brand or products is associated with a state of well-being and positivity, it will attract consumers who feel good when they buy a particular product.

Fig. 5.54. Use of happiness in a Coca Cola campaign.

Emotions and negative images, especially in fundraising, generally create a higher level of attention and generate more donations than campaigns and messages that use only positive emotions and images. However, the need or desire for a positive outcome is a necessary complement to negative emotions to activate a behaviour like making a donation. Donating to an organization, says Adrian Sargeant, becomes a way to overcome the negative emotions through positive outcomes, allowing us to imagine how it could have a positive finale.

In fundraising, positive emotions or happiness are essential in showing the response to negative emotions (sadness, anger, fear, disgust), or the need for which funds are collected. Positivity comes from showing how the donation can "buy" a solution or help to resolve the problem (e.g., "with your gift we can feed 10 children" or "we can guarantee drinking water to 250 people").

Happiness is also a fundamental emotion in the feedback and thank you to donors. The desire to know the outcome of the story (or "happy ending") increases both positive emotions and the donor response. According to Sargeant, to have greater impact, the thank you to donors after the first gift should refer to the original history, to the ambassador or to the example used in the first communication, in order to confirm the impact that the donation has had. We will come back to this aspect later, but it is important to note here that the satisfaction and happiness of customers is a key aspect of commercial business and should also be the main element of a fundraising approach that puts the donor at the centre of the relationship with the organization.

A good example of the use of positive emotions is one from charity: water. Its founder, Scott Harrison, strongly believes that the motivation to support a cause or an organization should not be the sense of guilt, but rather an opportunity to make a difference, to change a situation, and to save a life.[73]

73. Scott Harrison: "Why Charity Shouldn't Be About Guilt," September 24, 2011 http://www.inc.com/staff-blog/scott-harrison-why-charity-shouldnt-be-about-guilt-.html

Fig. 5.55. Use of happiness by charity:water.

The use of positive emotions, in particular through comedy and humour, can play a very important role in terms of audience involvement and fundraising. As mentioned earlier in this book, one of the pioneers of the use of comedy as opposed to other negative emotions is Comic Relief, a U.K. campaign conceived by film director Richard Curtis. This campaign aims to mobilize people to raise funds for a variety of social causes, associating fundraising with doing fun activities. The symbol of the campaign is in fact a red nose (Red Nose Day), a symbol that everyone can wear. At the close of the campaign—usually in April—a TV program on BBC with comedians and other celebrities invites viewers to donate to increase the target.

Fig. 5.56. Use of happiness by Comic Relief.

The mix between the performance of comedians, the report on the beneficiaries of donations and the use of emotionally strong videos (such as orphanages, hospitals with malaria victims, children and adolescents who attend sick relatives, etc.) have proven a winning combination. (For a summary of the model, see http://www.youtube.com/watch?v=Afq31vgo-nE&feature=player_embedded.)

Year	Date of TV Broadcast	BBC One Viewers	BBC Two Viewers	Total Funds Raised €
1999	12 March	6,830,000	3,130,000	€ 31,204,000
2001	16 March	8,510,000	N/A	€ 20,880,000
2003	14 March	11,740,000	6,010,000	€ 31,320,000
2005	11 March	10,940,000	4,720,000	€ 63,800,000
2007	16 March	9,730,000	6,400,000	€ 75,400,000
2009	13 March	9,840,000	7,090,000	€ 95,468,000
2011	18 March	10,260,000	7,530,000	€ 125,786,081

Fig. 5.57. Funds raised by Comic Relief.

The winning idea of the mix between comedy, humour and negative emotions related to difficult situations works in many other contexts. I personally have successfully exported this idea for UNICEF in Peru where the campaign "Buena Onda" (feeling/doing good) works with the same Anglo-Saxon model as inspiration. Buena Onda is a campaign with various popular comedians and fundraising activities, merchandising, corporate partnerships and a final TV program that combines reportage from the field, humour and celebrities. The campaign in 2009 has raised the equivalent of 1.5 million euros.

Fig. 5.58. Buena Onda.

ADVICE AND PRACTICAL TOOLS

Negative emotions are dominant in our behaviour and in our brains for biological and evolutionary reasons. The research in neuroscience and marketing and practical fundraising shows that these emotions work better to generate more responses to campaigns and appeals. However, when it comes to fundraising, combining this with positive emotions also has a crucial role in activating donors and supporters.

- Fear and sadness are very strong emotions that can mobilize many donors. Fear can generate responses by activating empathy with negative stories and conditions experienced by others or positioning a donor in the face of danger and risk that may affect him/her (e.g., violence, diseases, etc.). Guilt, when used with intelligence and integrity, can work well in fundraising, as in the successful example of Obama's digital campaign.

- Sadness activates mirror neurons through words and images, and can reactivate in our memories a nostalgic or melancholic mood that can stimulate the repeat of an action to make us feel better again. Nostalgia can play a very strong role in fundraising, particularly in promoting legacies

- Anger and disgust are two powerful emotions because of their primordial origin. These two emotions are frequently used by organizations such as Greenpeace and Amnesty International, and can be applicable to all causes to generate an immediate action-oriented response.

- Surprise is a fundamental emotion to attract attention and to anchor the message in the memory of the donors. However, surprise alone, or in the absence of a strong call to action, may not be effective because it can lead to paralysis and confusion.

- Happiness and positive emotions are key in fundraising if negative emotions are dominant in our brain. The use of humour and comedy mixed with, or opposed to, negative emotions are the basis of the formula for success of fundraising campaigns such as Comic Relief and Buena Onda.

Chapter 6

Ten techniques
and successful methods
for emotional fundraising

How to put emotionraising into practice? What methods and tools can help to ignite emotions in our donors? In this chapter, we will see ten techniques where emotions are key to influencing and persuading supporters and donors. These techniques and methods are the results of scientific research and studies that measured their validity, also in fundraising terms.

The main references of these ten emotionraising techniques derives from the work of four experts in psychology, communication and marketing: American psychologist Robert B. Cialdini[74], (note: Cialdini wrote a fascinating yet perhaps little-known essay that explains how the science of influence can be applied to fundraising[75]); communications gurus Dan and Chip Heath,[76] and Dan Hill, the pioneer of emotions in marketing and advertising. I added to their principles some fundraising applications derived from my practice and experience of 20 years. The ten successful techniques to get your audience and your supporters emotional are:

1. Reciprocity (you owe me a favour)

2. Scarcity or exclusivity (create something unique)

3. Authority (use the weight of the experience)

4. Consistency (one thing leads to another)

5. Sympathy (the power of those we like)

6. Imitation (the desire to follow others)

74. Robert B. Cialdini, Influence: *The Psychology of Persuasion,* Harper Business; Revised edition, 2006.
75. Robert B. Cialdini, "The Power of Persuasion: Putting the Science of Influence to Work in Fundraising," *Stanford Social Innovation Review,* 2006
76. Chip Heath, Dan Heath, *Made to Stick: Why Some Ideas Survive and Others Die,* Random House, 2007.

7. Authenticity (telling the truth is the trump card)

8. Transformation (the easiest way to show the difference)

9. Tangibility (focus on the concrete)

10. Urgency (we act only if it is an emergency or there is a deadline)

1. Reciprocity

Scarcity

The first principle identified by Cialdini is that of reciprocity and is based on the simple rule that when someone does something kind for us, or sends us a gift or a greeting card, we feel obliged to reciprocate. Cialdini mentions the experiment carried out in a restaurant where for several months they tried to understand why some waiters were able to get more tips. The waiters who offered a mint with the bill after a meal received 3 percent more tips; those who left two mints received 14 percent more, and those who, after a short break, returned to the table and offered free mints for all the guests, received 25 percent more. Therefore, an act of gratitude, a gift or a kind gesture activates a mechanism through which we feel "obliged" to do the same or to do something to replicate.

In marketing, this principle is often used with the use of premiums or discount vouchers. One of the funny anecdotes cited by Cialdini is the Ethiopian Red Cross, one of the poorest countries in the 1980s, which sent a donation of $5,000 to the Mexican Red Cross in aid for earthquake victims. The Red Cross of Ethiopia, despite being in a situation of relative poverty, felt "obliged" to help the Mexicans because they helped Ethiopia in 1935 when it was invaded by Italy!

In fundraising, especially in direct marketing, this principle is applicable to the use of premiums as an incentive to the donor. In a mailing, for example, that could be labels, postcards or other gadgets (e.g., plush animals for animal welfare or environmental organizations). Cialdini cites the case of the Disabled American Veterans who manages to get 35 percent of responses to its mailing using rewards and other incentives compared with 18 percent of responses to ordinary mailing.

Research on the effectiveness of premiums and gadgets in fundraising is ongoing, and the debate is very heated.[77] On the one hand, evidence shows that premiums help to get more responses to appeals because they work as incentives. Dan Shaw cites the cases of the Wilderness Society and the American Lung Association in the United States, who have tested the use of the premiums in two different groups of donors. Those who received a premium cost more (due to the

---

77. Dan Shaw, "Use of premiums in fundraising," http://happydonors.com/?p=522

cost of gadgets) and had a dropout rate higher than those who had only donated to the cause without premiums. However, both organizations considered the use of premiums a success because they had such a high volume of donations to cover the cost of premiums and the dropout of the donors after the first donation.

Roger Craver,[78] however, maintains that premiums are a kind of "drug" used to make the donor addicted to incentives instead of to the mission of the organization. Kevin Schuman[79] also mentions that motivating donors through benefits other than purely supporting a mission or cause can destroy the spirit and the emotional force that originally motivated the donor.

One way to use the principle of reciprocity is in the follow up to the donation—that is, from the moment we thank the donors for their first gift. At this stage, you can surprise the donor through messages and rewards to thank him/her for his/her contribution and strengthen the initial emotional bond. Videos and personalized photos from leadership or charity workers and beneficiaries, as well as other gadgets from the organization, can be used to enhance the relationship with the donor, strengthen his/her commitment to the cause and help generate other donations over time. Reciprocity strategies can include celebrating the birthday of the donor (both his/her real birthday and the years of participation with the organization's life). It can also include other unexpected experiences that create a bond of reciprocity based on the recognition and gratitude like phone calls, handwritten personalized messages, SMS and even visits and invitations to special events.

2. Scarcity or exclusivity

According to Cialdini, the limited availability of a product leads people to desire it more, because it is perceived as rare, restricted and therefore has a higher value. The shortage impairs our ability to think in a rational way and increases reliance on heuristic thought. In psychology, the scarcity heuristic is a mental shortcut that places a value on an item based on how easily it might be lost or how difficult it is to obtain, therefore making this item more valuable because it is limited.

This principle is often used in fundraising as a useful strategy to offer to a donor the opportunity to contribute to an exclusive goal or to a very limited project or edition. Through the segmentation of donors based on the level of

---

78. Roger Craver, "Acquisition: Premiums, Crack Cocaine And Nonprofit Suicide" http://www.thedonorvoice.com/non-profit-premiums-are-literally-crack-cocaine-the-why-and-how-of-stopping-the-drug-trade

79. Kevin Schulman, "Non Profit Premiums Are Literally Crack Cocaine – the Why and How of Stopping the 'Drug Trade,' February 6, 2013 http://www.thedonorvoice.com/non-profit-premiums-are-literally-crack-cocaine-the-why-and-how-of-stopping-the-drug-trade/

donation, you can identify a specific target (middle- and high-value donors) to send messages and targeted communications with exclusive offers to participate in and support campaigns and specific projects.

Scarcity can motivate donors to raise certain amounts (providing a minimum target) in exchange for which they have a specific and exclusive recognition—for example, a mention on a plaque on a physical structure, a building (e.g., hall of a museum) or on a website. Charity: water, for example, launches annual campaigns calling on its supporters to donate to a project through their birthday party, inviting their friends to donate instead of making gifts. Those who collect at least $25,000 receive a dedicated plaque with thanks on the water pump that the organization will build.

Fig. 6.59. Use of exclusivity by charity:water.

This practice, called "naming rights," is very common in the United States and England (where it was initiated by sports marketing), and is particularly used by universities and museums working with businesses and major donors. In practice, especially in capital campaigns, in which an organization needs substantial capital to build new infrastructures, prospective donors, according to their level of donations, can to put their name in the main hall (e.g. Paul Hamlyn in London's Royal Opera House) or can associate their name to a professorship, a library or to a university faculty.

The principle of scarcity or exclusivity also works in digital platforms and crowdfunding sites like Kickstarter, where exclusive levels of bonuses and awards are granted depending on the level of contribution.

3. Authority

This principle, mentioned by Cialdini and the Heath brothers, explains why certain messages become memorable, if originated by an authoritative source. Our brain believes in and obeys someone with authority, whether real or imagined. This is why we automatically pay attention to someone who wears a white coat in a hospital or feel more secure if a so-called expert sponsors a product. Many organizations have experienced and credible people on their boards or as ambassadors who can add credibility and give authority to our messages and to our fundraising.

According to Dan and Chip Heath, there are various ways to make a credible message. They proposed the "Frank Sinatra tests" as a verification tool. In the famous song, the lyrics "If I can make it there, I'll make it anywhere" exemplifies that if you can prove that you have overcome challenges in many critical situations, you are credible and authoritative.

An example, according to Heath brothers, that passes the Sinatra Test is that if you've got the security contract for Fort Knox, you're in the running for any security contract (even if you have no other clients). If you catered a White House function, you can compete for any catering contract.

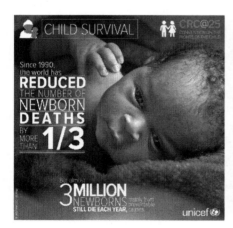 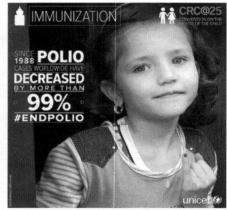

Fig. 6.60. Examples of UNICEF "saving children."

Although we saw that images and stories of individual cases work better in fundraising than numbers and figures, the use of details and statistics can help make our message more credible. In a study mentioned by Cialdini, for example, jurors are more likely to trust parents of a child who tell many details, although irrelevant, of that child instead of parents who talk generically about a child.

Statistics and details, especially in social media, serve to give credibility and authority. Statistics and details are very useful both on Twitter and through infographics when trying represent the needs and activities of nonprofit organizations in an authoritative and understandable manner. But more important, examples of relevant and notable achievements, services, or partners your organization has worked with or for can help you stand out from the crowd of other nonprofits.

Having verifiable credentials is essential in making a donor feel at ease. Make sure you publish your annual general accounts and expenses, especially online, and get certifications such as the "Charity Navigator," which can give some confidence and authority. An example of fundraising that uses authority is adapted from the principle of the marketing "money back guarantee" (from the Showcase of Fundraising Innovation and Inspiration (SOFII) http://sofii.org/case-study/habitat-for-humanity-money-back-guarantee).

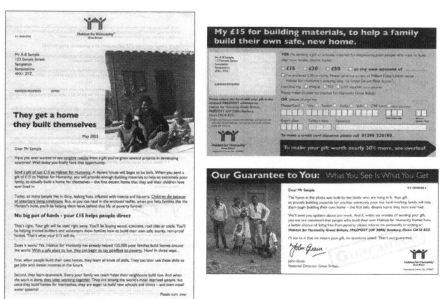

Fig. 6.61. Example of a mailing from Habitat for Humanity.

The fundraising campaign by Habitat for Humanity tested this principle: a group of donors received a regular donation request, and another group received an additional guarantee that they could request money back if not satisfied by information received, or if he/she believed that the organization did not use the donation properly or efficiently. The result was that the two groups responded in the same percentage, but the group that received the "money back" guarantee made donations for a value of 50 percent higher on average than the other group. Moreover, and most important, no one asked the money back.

4. Consistency

We behave consistently with our past behaviour: what we said, what we did, what people think of us are important to us. According to Cialdini, the main factor that motivates people to be consistent with their actions is that we do not want to be seen as inconsistent with our past actions.

This is particularly important in making a second donation, and in increasing the donation in the future. Fundraising has understood that very often it is easier to ask someone to make a non-financial commitment—e.g. sign a petition, send an email, engage their friends on Facebook—and then later ask to turn this commitment into a financial contribution. We have already seen it previously, as the Obama campaign used history of previous donations as an element of success, relying on the sense of donor guilt and when the consistency of what we did as donors is called into question.

In fundraising, which derives this principle from marketing, the category of people who want to "first try and then buy" has been called the "trysummers".[80] These consumers are very likely, once they have had the chance to experience a service, a product or an organization, to turn into consumers or loyal and regular donors. Marcelo Iniarra and Alfredo Botti, formerly of Greenpeace, tested this principle. In 2007, Greenpeace in Argentina had a base of about 200,000 activists (trysummers) but they were not active. They involved them in a campaign to pass legislation to protect forests, and Greenpeace was able to transform 70,000 of these activists into donors who contributed with over 2.5 million euros to Greenpeace in 2008.

This is also why it costs ten times more to acquire a new donor than to convince an existing one— or, even more difficult, to ask lapsed donors to donate again.

5. Sympathy

The sympathy principle is based on the pressure or influence of people around us (friends, relatives, etc.). Cialdini's example is Tupperware, which bases its marketing strategy on activation of housewives and their friends through organized events on their premises, where the cordial and friendly atmosphere will also sell

---

80. Marcelo Iniarra, "Social trysumers and the free experience era." October 13, 2010 http://sofii-foundation. blogspot.ch/2010/10/social-trysumers-and-free-experience.html

products. Various market research has shown that 67 percent of all buying is based on word of mouth and, as mentioned in the first part of this book, donations are activated by mirror neurons and empathy: we are more likely to donate to causes and organizations supported by people who we like or trust and that are doing something we feel we should also do.

In recent years, several successful campaigns used this principle: charity: water asks its supporters to donate their on birthday; the Movember campaign against prostate cancer asks participants to grow a moustache in November and raise funds; Merlin invites its supporters to survive a week eating only the Plumpy'nut (an energy food used against malnutrition) and to raise donations for this.

Fig. 6.62. Movember campaign and use of sympathy.

The principle of sympathy extends to "role models" and celebrities or testimonials, and applies especially to social media. Dan Zarrella[81] recently conducted a study of more than 1.2 million updates on the most popular 10,000 Facebook pages and found that the updates with the most engagement were those who had a clear "call to action" (write, share, whether you like it or not). Dan suggests that phrases like "leave a comment," "like this post" and "share this message" can have a huge impact to stimulate the commitment of Facebook fans and visitors.

81. Dan Zarrella, "New Facebook data proves social CTAs lead to more comments, likes & shares," November 20, 2012 http://blog.hubspot.com/blog/tabid/6307/bid/33860/New-Facebook-Data-Proves-Social-CTAs-Lead-to-More-Comments-Likes-Shares-INFOGRAPHIC.aspx

6. Imitation or social proof

Cialdini describes this principle as replicating the behaviour and actions of others like us. It is important in fundraising that a donor feels or perceives him/herself to be part of a greater community of donors, and that they are not the only donor. For example, in capital campaigns the rule 80/20 or 90/20 means that you have to secure at least 80 percent of the initial capital target, through promises of gifts from major donors or companies, before launching a public campaign.

The message, "We need $10 million. We have already raised $80 million… help us to achieve our goal" is more effective than, "We need $10 million more; help us." The same principle applies in television campaigns like telethons in which you ensure at least 70 percent of the resources before the program, showing therefore that contributions received gradually during the show support the collective effort to reach the final target—ideally, an amount higher than the total raised in the previous year.

One mistake we make often is using the imitation principle as negative. Psychologists Noah Goldstein and Steve Martin[82] have observed such effects in advertising campaigns. The results were surprising. For example, in the case of a famous public park, a sign saying that there were many visitors who stole memorabilia such as stones and other objects actually encouraged more thefts because the sign was proof that many other people were already stealing, which paradoxically convinced visitors that stealing was quite acceptable. Other examples of the use of negative social proof in public campaigns that have the opposite effect to the intentions are as follows:

- "Four years ago, over 22 million women did not vote."
- "This year Americans will produce more waste and pollution than ever."
- "Our heritage is the victim of vandalism every day because of the theft of about 14 tons of our petrified wood per year."

These campaigns seek to argue that a certain behaviour is "wrong", but they do it by saying that many people are doing it—paradoxically making the behaviour they fight legitimate. This principle works when used positively and showing that many others follow the desirable behaviour. For example, to persuade the public to make less use of air conditioning and less energy in the summer, the researchers tested four types of messages:

1. "Using less air conditioning can save $54 a month on your bill."

---

82. Steve J. Martin; Noah Goldstein; Robert Cialdini: *The Small BIG: Small Changes that Spark Big Influence*, Grand Central Publishing, 2014

2. "Using less air conditioning means that 262 fewer pounds of greenhouse gas will be released into the air each month."

3. "Energy saving is a socially responsible action."

4. "77 percent of your neighbours are using fans instead of air conditioning, saving them a lot of energy and a lot of money."

What was the most effective message in getting people to use less energy? The fourth, because it used positive imitation mechanisms. In this case, most of the messages were focused on money and responsible choices, all of which are positive behaviours, but the fourth message works because it leverages the power of similar behaviour among human beings.

The principle of imitation works even in so-called peer-to-peer fundraising, or in fundraising which utilized social networks (community, families, friends, etc.). Influence fundraising works because the 71.7 percent of the so-called "Millennial donors"[83] or young generations, say they want to involve friends and family in support to organizations to which they donate and would donate more to organizations suggested by family members (74.6 percent) and friends (62.8 percent).

7. Authenticity

Authenticity is one of the core elements of the globalized world. According to Joseph Pine and James Gilmore,[84] authenticity is so central in our lives because it is part of the "economy of experience." Goods and services are no longer sufficient; what consumers want today are memorable experiences, events involving them in an inherently personal way. Bombarded by the proliferation of experiences, the consumer decides when and where to spend their money and their time, and evaluates the experience more than the product itself. Consumers choose to buy based on how authentic they perceive an offer or a product. To succeed as a company or as a nonprofit in the world today, according to Pine and Gilmore, you have to be perceived as real, genuine, honest and authentic.

Today, donors are more informed and have more means. They are surrounded by thousands of causes and requests for funds, and want to connect with those organizations that they perceived as genuine. In short, like the Bible's St. Thomas, they want to see and touch to believe.

Initiatives such as child sponsorship—four million children are estimated

---

83. www.millennialdonors.com

84. James H. Gilmore; B. Joseph Pine: *Authenticity: What Consumers Really Want*, Harvard Business School Press, 2007.

to be sponsored, generating $8 billion a year—or micro-credit and other micro-funding (such as crowdfunding or Kickstarter) connect the donor directly with the beneficiary, and their growing popularity is due to the capacity of promoting the authenticity of their causes.

In the case of child sponsorship, indeed we do help a cause or an organization to support a child, a family or a specific village; we can see the photos, we can receive letters and reports on their lives, etc. The same true for micro-credit: we receive regular updates on how loans are used and, once the loan is paid off, we can decide whether to allocate it to others or not.

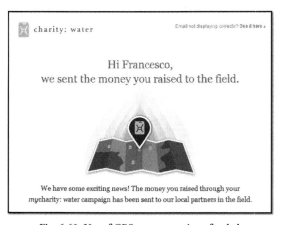

Fig. 6.63. Use of GPS to trace projects funded.

Mainly thanks to new web-based technologies, it is now possible to locate the effect and the destination of the funds using GPS or Google Maps in real time. Organizations like charity: water offer the possibility of locating the project to which you contribute via GPS coordinates, while one of the main micro-credit organizations, KIVA, provides clear representations of flows between donors and recipients.

How do we make our fundraising authentic? By exploiting the potential of new technologies and providing messages and images that are verifiable and direct. Here are some examples.

Traceability: Not all donors have the time, the means or the desire to go personally to check the results of what organizations do with their donations. However, as noted above, new technologies now make it possible to show both where our projects are located, and enable the donor to see, should they wish, the implementation of our campaigns or the situations of the people we want to help. Using digital technology there are endless possibilities:

- GPS and Google maps can locate interventions and projects;
- Live feeds and Web cameras can show what is happening in real time;
- Photographs of field workers and beneficiaries can be seen;
- Videos in real time—testimonials, donors or celebrities—can be seen.

In addition to social media, the same experience may also be communicated offline through letters and reports.

Service for **competent and active donors**. Authenticity can be enhanced through a 24/7 service for active donors/supporters— one that responds in real time to donors' questions and requests. We will see in Chapter 8 how UNICEF's approach of speed and authenticity led to saving millions of Euros and regaining thousands of potentially dissatisfied donors.

No intermediaries. Another key to authenticity is giving donors the chance to receive feedback and information directly from beneficiaries or field workers (doctors, teachers, etc.) and staff. Communications, online and off, by all staff to donors offer a great opportunity to make our messages credible and authentic.

8. Transformation

One of the ways to use the force of emotions is to show the "before and after" of the action of your organization. In marketing, this principle works; whether it's a diet or a car, we are amazed and excited to see the transformation before and after a wash with a soap or the application of a drop of glue. We don't have to be interested in the product or service to appreciate the before and after images. Watching the transformation is a powerful emotional mechanism that potentially attracts a customer to buy a product or to participate in an initiative.

Many organizations aim to transform or improve situations and therefore can use the before and after mechanism with great effectiveness. Organizations like Operation Smile use this principle in a very effective way.

Fig. 6.64. Use of transformation by Operation Smile.

It works very well during emergencies or in the construction of physical infrastructure (hospitals, schools or universities) because it shows the progress of a project. However, this is not always possible for more complex situations or ones that require a long period of time to show changes or improvements. In those cases, you can still imagine the "after" scenario: imagine the situation of this child, village, school, hospital if we could build, deliver, cure, etc. Girl Effect and similar campaigns use the "after" as an ideal world possible thanks to the donations from supporters.

Here are some suggestions for using this mechanism effectively:

- Try to show similar images; do not let the audience become distracted by details. If you show a house or a person before, then show the same house or person after.
- Make sure that the result, or the "after," is shown in a similar size to the "before" image. The car, house, body, etc., should be the same size in both.
- Allow the pictures to dominate the words, address or telephone number. Photos capture our attention and make us want to know more. Don't let the transformation shown in the images get lost in a sea of words and numbers.

9. Tangibility

This principle is suggested by Dan and Chip Heath to create a memorable message. As we have seen, our brain is hard-wired to react and remember images and other sensory stimuli (colours, smells, tastes, and objects) rather than words. Non-profit organizations tend to use terminology, acronyms and statistics, or technical terms difficult to understand by non-experts. If ordinary people do not understand, then the emotional part of their brain is not active and therefore does not issue the "order" of take an action like donating. We have seen how the different senses are involved in activating emotions. The tactile part in particular is closely linked with emotional mechanisms. Physically touching an object allows you to elicit some emotions.

Tangibility in fundraising is crucial and a good fundraiser obsessively seeks tangible examples to explain their causes and activities. In 2006, Procter and Gamble launched a campaign, in partnership with UNICEF, to increase the sales of Pampers diapers with the slogan, "A pack of diapers = one vaccine" to help eliminate tetanus, a major cause of infant mortality. This was one of the most successful campaigns for P&G in terms of brand awareness and sales. The same campaign, but with the generic slogan, "A pack of diapers helps eliminate tetanus among newborns at the global level," has not been equally effective. Why? The first message has emotional tangibility.

In one experiment, Cynthia Cryder and George Loewenstein[85] asked two different groups to donate to OXFAM. The first group received materials explaining how concretely the donation will support the distribution of drinking water in West Africa, while a second group received a generic description of OXFAM activities. Obviously, the first group donated, on average, more than twice what the second group donated.

"GENERAL" CONDITION	"TANGIBLE" CONDITION
Oxfam International is one of the most effective aid organizations in the world. Oxfam provides a broad range of aid to people across the globe. Any donation that you make will go directly towards one of Oxfam's greatest needs	Oxfam International is one of the most effective aid organizations in the world. One example of how Oxfam provides aid is ensuring that villagers in West Africa have access to clean water. Any donation that you make will go directly towards one of Oxfam's greatest needs

Condition	Amount donated	Sympathy	Vividness	Impact
General	$7.54a	5.04a	3.5a	5.0a
Details—high impact	$10.25b	5.25b	4.6b	5.6b
Details—low impact	$6.95a	5.38b	4.6b	5.1a

Fig. 6.65. Donation amount based on tangible impact (Cryder, Loewenstein, Scheines, 2013).

In a similar experiment, "Nothing But Nets," an organization that buys mosquito nets to protect against malaria, received more than three times the number of donations with a tangible appeal compared to a generic Oxfam appeal. Even though Oxfam is a well-known household brand, donors still respond better to emotional mechanisms like tangibility.

The tangibility of problems and proposed solutions is fundamental in convincing and exciting donors. We have already talked about the success of the UNICEF campaign with ORS sachets and malnutrition-measuring arm bracelets.

Another example of the use of the tangibility is when Bill Gates conveyed to his audience at a TED Talk an understanding of what malaria is by opening a jar and freeing dozens of mosquitoes (which had, of course, been previously sterilized in a laboratory).

85. Cryder, Cynthia E.; & Loewenstein, George; Scheines, Richard: "The donor is in the details," Organizational Behavior and Human Decision Processes, Elsevier, 2013, vol. 120(1), pages 15-23.

Fig. 6.66. Bill Gates at TED.

Tangibility attaches things to our memory like Velcro. Our brains don't store information like a repository, with folders classified under certain categories. Rather our brains anchor information in various sections already present. Using tangible items like objects, pictures and words helps our brain to anchor messages to emotions, memories and images.

10. Urgency

Many fundraisers know that suggesting a deadline, evoking an urgency or an emergency, has an important effect on donations. In fact, if a cause or a situation is not urgent, why we should rush to donate? Natural disasters trigger the greatest fundraising results. Jonathon Grapsas[86] argues that the urgency of our demands in fundraising is a key element in enabling donors.

Grapsas suggests three ways in which you can use an emergency in fundraising:

1. Use a deadline. "If you send us your donation by June 30 we could support/help…"

2. Be mindful of tone and language. There's no need to be over the top, but try to connect the need for funds to a real person, and make the situation dramatic in order to support the need to act now.

3. Repeat the message, typically at least five or six times on one page

---

86. Jonathon Grapsas, "Is your appeal urgent?" April 7, 2010 http://jonathongrapsas.blogspot.ch/2010/04/is-your-appeal-urgent.html

4. What are the consequences if we fail to raise the necessary funds? There is no need to dramatize this, but do highlight the negative effects that a late or slow response could have; it will help make the sense of urgency more real.

An example of how urgency works is the so-called "matching mechanism." We previously secure a commitment from a company and major donor and then we invite others to donate, explaining that every donation received by a certain date will be doubled thanks to the company's or major donor's contribution. A U.S. UNICEF campaign in partnership with Kimberly Clark suggested that every donation will be doubled ,thanks to a sponsor, and indicates a deadline. This campaign raised 50 percent more donations, with an average gift of at least 5 percent higher compared to the same campaign without a deadline.

Fig. 6.67. Use of urgency in U.S. Fund for UNICEF.

In UNICEF in Italy, thanks to a partnership with PayPal, we invited customers to become a Friend of UNICEF (Fig. 66), i.e., a monthly donor, with the idea that for every new donor PayPal would donate the equivalent of a week of therapeutic food for children. We managed to get 600 new monthly donors in few weeks.

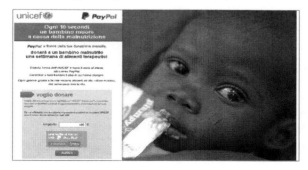

Fig. 6.68. Friend of UNICEF.

ADVICE AND PRACTICAL TOOLS

Ten techniques can help to develop more emotional and more effective fundraising. Based on experts in psychology, communications and marketing such as Robert Cialdini, Dan and Chip Heath and Dan Hill, these principles are very effective in fundraising.

Reciprocity. Create a feeling of obligation by sending an unexpected gift or a "thank you" for a donor's support. Beyond the use of premiums and gadgets, whose effectiveness is still unclear in fundraising, surprising the donor with a personalized communication based on gratitude for his/her donation or celebrating important events and achievements during donor lifetime significantly increases the value of donations and loyalty over time.

Scarcity. Provide donors with "exclusive offers" and specific awards (a mention on your website or in the annual report, the chance to participate in special events and visits), helps to increase the level of donations and loyalty over time.

Authority. Use the so-called "Frank Sinatra test" (if you have been successful in a difficult place, you can succeed anywhere) and use verifiable credentials—statistics or experts—to help make messages credible and authoritative. In particular, the "money-back guarantee" formula can deliver solid results and add credibility.

Consistency. Getting commitments, including non-financial actions such as signing petitions or volunteering, helps in transforming occasional partici-pants into regular donors. The so-called "trysummers"—those who want to experience before making a donation—are more inclined to donate after they sign a petition or perform similar non-monetary acts.

Sympathy. One of the most powerful mechanisms to donate is the pressure or influence of the people around us (friends, relatives, etc.).

Imitation or social proof. There are behaviours and actions we like to imitate if we see others like us perform them.

Authenticity. Modern consumers are seeking unique experiences more than products or brands. A way to make our appeals more authentic is to use real-time information, images and traceable communications (GPS and Google maps) to connect donors directly to beneficiaries.

Transformation. "Before and after" always works in activating emotional mechanisms, especially with images.

Tangibility. Using objects, or evoking them through images and words, to activate the tactile senses can make a strong connection between a donor and a cause/organization. The ORS sachet and malnutrition bracelet are good examples of tangible fundraising.

Urgency. Building a sense of urgency or putting a deadline to our fundraising increases responses to our fundraising.

Chapter 7

Emotionraising with the general public, with business and with major donors

Many of the examples might suggest that emotions are fundraising devices only for individuals via mass marketing channels such as direct mail, TV, face to face, and so on.

While emotions undoubtedly play a decisive role in convincing individuals to donate, they are also a key element in fundraising with corporations, foundations and major donors.

It is true that when it comes to fundraising work with institutions, the rational factors are very important: the project, the framework, the guidelines and the form. But it is also true that much of the success of a proposal or a partnership relies on establishing a relationship with individual decision makers—the CEO, VPs, managers, boards, etc. For this reason, the same rules and techniques that apply to the general public are also relevant for corporations, foundations and major donors.

Foundations and companies have their target audience (customers, shareholders, employees and founders). Therefore, they are looking to identify emotional experiences to which they can associate their brand, their audiences and their communications.

An example of how emotions are important also in fundraising with institutional players can be seen in the process through which projects are selected by foundations. According to experts, a foundation receives an average of 20-30 funding proposals every day (this varies between the U.S. and Europe). These proposals are usually divided into three groups: 60 percent that are immediately rejected; 40 percent that are considered potentially fundable; and, of the latter, 10 percent that are actually funded. Proposals are rejected for formal "rational" reasons—for example, they are centred on themes and issues outside of then foundation's established priorities, they contain typos, they are addressed to the wrong person, etc.

However, among the proposals that could be relevant because they are close to the foundation's priorities, the main obstacle is often that they are too technical, or do not make clear the problem they want to address. Experts say that the main purpose of a call for proposals is to convince the foundation that your project addresses a specific need, a dramatic and urgent issue that matches what the foundation is passionate about. So in the end it is the emotional need we have to express when we make an appeal! Once more, rules and relevance to rational guidelines are key to succeeding with foundations, but human relationships are also critically important, such as between board members and officers. Therefore, emotion is still the key.

Emotions, brands and businesses

A second area where the power of emotions is vastly underestimated is corporate fundraising. We have already seen in the first part of this book that most commercial advertising has now veered completely into emotional content because companies understand that the consumer's actions and decisions are guided by the emotional part of the brain. TV spots during the Super Bowl (for example, and as already noted, where companies spent over US$2 billion in the past ten years and where a 30-second spot costs about US$4 million), are designed with an emotional approach in mind. But there is more: the association of a brand with a social cause (so-called cause-related marketing) has become less marginal and is an essential part of marketing strategies that companies need to have if they want to be able succeed in an increasingly competing world.

For example, in research conducted by Edelman on the perception of the association between a product and a good cause, consumers who think that an association with a good cause is essential when buying a product or brand rose from 42 percent to 53 percent in the past few years.

If buying and branding are essentially based on emotions, nonprofits have a lot to offer in terms of content and experience for a solid partnership—without selling their soul.

Fig. 7.69. The rise of cause-related marketing and emotional buying.
Edelman goodpurpose® 2012 Global Consumer Survey.

Chapter 8

Emotional loyalty and donor love

Emotions are also the key for a healthy, long-term sustainable relationship with donors.

There are some statistics and numbers that stick with you for months and constantly challenge your assumptions. One that keeps me awake at night (seriously!) is the ratio 6:59. Yes, you know, or you should know, that this is the percentage of customer attrition in the commercial world vs. the nonprofit sector, according to Bloomerang.

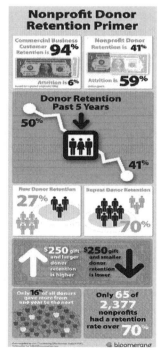

Fig. 8.70. Retention in nonprofits.

We can discuss the sample or the methodology and argue that this does not represent our average charity or our country, but you would admit that the gap is so wide (6:59!) that we need to ask why we lose most of our donors (and we know that a large majority of our first-time donors will not repeat their gift) and yet business is able to keep most of their customers. I am not a fan of the idea that "business does it better" but would like to use some real-life stories to understand where and how business increasingly invests in creating emotionally engaged customers as a key driver of their financial bottom line, compared to our world, where retention and attrition are still big headaches.

One of the key insights[87] discovered in the commercial world is that emotionally satisfied customers are substantially more profitable compared to rationally satisfied or dissatisfied customers.

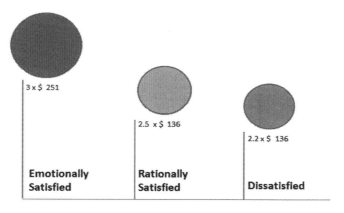

Fig. 8.71. Emotionally satisfied customers are more valuable than rationally satisfied. B. Pearson, *The Loyalty Leap*, Penguin.

Sounds easy or obvious? Let's see what is happening in the real world.

My experience with loyalty

One day, years ago when I was working at a big INGO, I heard loud voices shouting and arguing in the lobby of our building. Being curious, I got closer and I heard that the security guards at the entrance were having an animated discussion with an elderly couple. The guards were saying that they couldn't let them in because they didn't have ID and didn't know who they were. As the discussion went on, I realized they were major donors to our organization and that they had

---

87. Brian Pearson, *The Loyalty Leap: Turning Customer Information into Customer Intimacy*, Portfolio; 1st edition, 2012

come for a meeting. They were about to leave because they felt mistreated. I went to the guards, explained the situation, and escorted the couple into the building. Results: a substantial donation and a donor relationship were saved by chance. This episode makes me think of how many donors we leave at the door, waiting on the telephone or trying to connect with us, in vain, on our web page. It also makes me think of how of many of our front-line staff (operators, security guards, janitors, doormen, etc.) are aware of the importance and relevance of donors to the organization. Then I look at the commercial world and can see that the standard there is set by companies like Zappos (now acquired by Amazon): the secret of their financial success is that each employee, especially in the customer care department and call centre, is empowered to do anything—including spend money without manager authorization—to make a customer happy, to the point that if you call them and ask where a Taco Bell is open at 1 a.m. in a given locality, they will find out for you, even if you don't buy anything from Zappos!

The second story is about the painful experience of trying to get things fixed through customer or donor service. Years ago, when I was in London and moving from one flat to another, I called British telecom to get my telephone line transferred. The critical utility you need the most is an Internet connection, and you can have that only if you have a telephone line. Of course, commercial companies don't always get it right. So, after some painful calls to the customer service centre with no luck, I googled "CEO BT" and "email," found his email address and sent him an email with the subject "BT customer care: a joke!" Five minutes later I received the following email from Sir Ian Livingston, CEO of BT, who is today Minister for Trade in the U.K. government.

```
Subject: RE: BT and customer service: a joke!
Date: Thu, 3 Sep 2009 08:52:16 +0100
From: ian.livingston@bt.com
To: ambrogetti_f@hotmail.com
CC: elc@bt.com; warren.buckley@bt.com; stephen.wade@bt.com

I am sorry about the problems you have had. I will ask one of our high
level service team to look into it and contact you to resolve matters.

Ian Livingston


-----Original Message-----
From: Ambrogetti Francesco Saverio [mailto:ambrogetti_f@hotmail.com]
Sent: 03 September 2009 08:44
To: Livingston,I,Ian,CGEC R
Cc: Suzanne
Subject: BT and customer service: a joke!

Dear Mr. Livingston,

After been for a year a customer of BT we moved flat and we naively
thought that we can transfer our telephone line and broad band internet
at the new address. Obviously not because you have first to activate a
new line and after that you can order a broad band.
```

Fig. 8.72. Email acknowledgement and customer service from BT .

The next day, the line was installed, and when I sent an email to thank him, he personally thanked me for letting him know there was a problem, and apologized for my experience. And this example isn't just a lucky one; I repeated the same experiment with other companies (banks, credit cards, magazines, telephone, etc.) in U.K., Panama and Switzerland and got problems fixed, received compensations—and rewards—and several apologies. So, when you've got a problem, go straight to the CEO. Don't waste your time with customer service.

But how can I compare this experience with several frustrating attempts to get engaged with a charity? Years ago I donated to what I believed was one of the best and most compelling campaigns I had ever seen. I donated not just because I am a fundraiser, but because I was so moved and convinced that my contribution would make a difference for an ambitious but possible target. This organization's income went from $12 million to $28 million overnight and recruited hundreds of thousands of new regular donors, most of them young. After a year of regular monthly giving through my credit card I wrote to them with anger and disappointment, explaining I hadn't received any communications from them for a year. The response I got back is below.

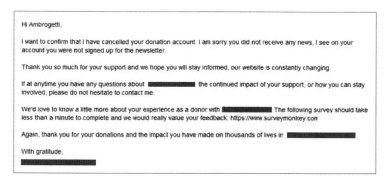

Fig 8.73. Email acknowledgement and donor service from Invisible Children.

Let's have a look:
- "Hi Ambrogetti." (Nice to be called by my last name, and without even a Mr.!)
- It is my fault because I didn't sign up for the newsletter. (!!)
- I can go on their website to stay informed. (I just wrote to say I am upset because I didn't hear anything from you!!!!)
- I can get in touch if I have questions about their work. (I just did it !!!!!!!)
- They would love to hear about my donor experience, so I should take a survey. (Are you joking!!!!!!!???????)

If we really want to resolve the puzzle of 6:59 and start making money for our causes, we should consider the following strategic points:

- Let's turn around the basic assumptions and the budgets: retention is the new acquisition! So let's invest accordingly, devote teams and people to it and reward them: if they are happy, donors are happy.
- Emotions drive human decisions, including the decision to give again and stay with a charity. Therefore, we should invest in more emotional engagement with donors AFTER the donations, not only when we acquire new donors.
- Be sure that your CEO and your Board have regular access to emails, calls and letters from donors, especially when they complain.

Emotional loyalty?

The malaise of fundraising about donor attrition, the donor churn rate or the fact that donors leave organizations after a few donations is a well-known dilemma (among many; see Roger Craver[88] and Tom Belford,[89] and also the rants of Lucy Gower[90] and Reiner Spruit[91]). Notwithstanding their "prescriptions" on donor's loyalty and relationship, by Adrian Sargeant[92] and Ken Burnett, we still sadly look mainly at the number. Call it retention or attrition, loyalty or stewardship, donors are leaving us.

We know the data; on average, and depending on the market, we can lose between 30 percent and 80 percent of first-time donors (in some cases, such as face to face, that can even happen within the first 12 months). Meanwhile, the commercial sector loses only 6 percent. Only a limited number of existing donors (20 percent to 30 percent) give more than once a year. And this is not just the average donor. In the U.S., 30 percent of high-net-worth donors stop supporting at least one organization, and 32 percent stop giving to two organizations.

We all know the basic cure: a (personalized?) welcome note, email or call, and a personal thank you to donors, showing them the impact and the difference their gift make, engaging them in various activities such as inviting them to events and field visits. So why don't they stay, and why don't they give again?

I argue that the answer to retention is not only a well-executed donor care

88. http://www.theagitator.net/uncategorized/fundraising-intermission-1-retention-again/?utm_source=rss&utm_medium=rss&utm_campaign=fundraising-intermission-1-retention-again
89. http://www.theagitator.net/uncategorized/the-fundraising-cliff/
90. http://101fundraising.org/2013/01/this-blog-is-a-bit-of-a-rant/
91. http://101fundraising.org/2013/01/knock-knock-whos-there-opportunity/
92. Adrian Sargeant; Elaine Jay: *Building Donor Loyalty: The Fundraiser's Guide to Increasing Lifetime Value*, Jossey-Bass, 2011.

program (although we can and must always improve!), and of course finding the right target audience to begin with, but it is about improving the emotional gap with our donors. Think about it. Our first meeting with donors (our "first date") is all about emotional engagement: we have the power to trigger powerful emotions like anger, fear, and sadness and we make feel people happy through their gift. This is thanks to the incredible experience that a donor lives through a myriad of senses stimulated by the power of the stories we tell with our images, sounds and words. And what happens next? They receive a (personalized?) thank you letter or a note (maybe a call or an email), some newsletters or a glossy report, more appeals and requests for funds or requests to increase their donation. Like in the saddest love stories, the spark of the first date is gone—there is no more emotion in our relationship. Therefore, many donors look for other experiences or new relationships.

Many fundraisers believe that a prompt acknowledgment and a "thanks for the donation," a regular update on what the donation has helped to achieve (and don't forget to ask again!) will ensure a donors stay with us forever. They are wrong.

Part of the problem of donor disconnect is in that formulaic approach fundraisers use (like the £3 a month offer popular in the U.K.; the welcome pack; the reactivation of lapsed donors email; etc.). In fact, it is often the formula that, just like the "output" of a production process, has little effect—or even a negative effect—on donor loyalty.

If you really want to know why the majority of donors leave and how to regain their love, read Roger Craver's book and apply the variety of tools and suggestions.[93]

But I also want to focus on three mysterious ways, often ignored, that make donors feel ignored, abandoned or mistreated by charities, and what in the end leads them to "break up" with us and start dating somebody else (can you blame them?). Then I'll suggest some ideas for what to do about it, rather than just complaining or contemplating the fact that our donors are leaving.

The "would-be" donor

The first fact is, in my opinion, the widely unrecognized and unaddressed would-be donors. These are donors who agreed to donate (especially on a regular monthly basis) but for whom we cannot process the payments.

---

93. Roger Craver., *Retention Fundraising: The New Art and Science of Keeping Your Donors for Life*, Emerson & Church Publishers, 2014.

The majority of charities are defining their retention based on the time from the first gift—for example, those who don't give after three to six months (or another time measure). But what about those who agree in principle to become a donor, but never gave? This is a large number of people, especially those recruited via face to face, but also through DRTV and online, who are often simply "ditched" after we try to charge their credit/debit card or bank account once, twice or three times.

What really struck me is that we consider this issue as simply a transactional problem and leave it to the administration and finance people, or to the backup office/agency, and we do not investigate the causes and the alternatives to fulfill the donor's pledge. Even more worrying is the assumption of the fundraisers that these people never really intended to give—that they said they want to give, but they did not really want to, or they cannot afford it. See how the theory works? You agree to give, you give me the bank details, I will try to charge you and if it doesn't work (after several attempts), I am sorry you are not a donor.

The result is that would-be donors don't even get put into retention calculations or future strategies. However, there are so many reasons and opportunities that are worth considering before dropping them. In fact, the inability to get the donation can be related to many factors: credit cards or debit cards have cutoff dates (so we can perhaps offer different payment or collection dates); people use multiple payment systems (are we bothering to ask them for a second or a third card, or a different account?); or there is simply no money in that account this month but there will be in the next month or two (making it also possible to recoup the missing payments).

If we can transform 10 percent to 20 percent of these would-be donors into actual donors, with minimum effort, we will substantially increase our income even before we start looking at retention figures.

In UNICEF Italy we implemented a plan for would-be donors and we saved millions of dollars a year, just interacting with and listening to them, working to solve the transaction problems and negotiating different terms.

"Donor sapiens"

The second part of the problem is that fundraisers know very well that emotions drive people to act and to donate, and that in fact they spend most of their resources in conceiving appeals, looking for stories and finding the right words, images or videos to trigger the donor's emotions to engage with their cause. But after donors give for the first time, it's like they are dealing with a different species of donors: "donor sapiens."

These particular creatures, according to a stereotypical idea of the donor, are always well-informed because they read the newsletter and go to website; they donate on time and they know when to renew their gift; they are altruistic, so they don't need to be thanked; they clearly know that we have to cover our overhead costs and are happy to be over-solicited; they enthusiastically engage their friends in the causes they support; etc.

I am afraid these donors do not exist in nature, or they are very few. The majority of donors are very much limited in their attention and memory. In fact, what fundraisers often ignore is that emotions not only drive actions (and donations) but also strongly contribute to memory formation, so that every time a donor gets in contact with our cause, he or she is expecting to be engaged by the same emotions, not by our organizational blurbs.

If you look closely to the reasons why donors stop giving, you can bet that you will see several mentions of the fact that they have no memory of supporting such organizations or they thought we did not need their support!

In the business world, there is a clear understanding that today's profit margins rely heavily on the level of customer emotional engagement. If you have not seen the campaign "TD Bank Turns ATMs into Automated Thanking Machines," have a close look. The beauty of this campaign is that it's not just another PR campaign. It is part of a clear strategy to get more enthusiastic customers who will love TD Bank and do more business with it. As its then-CEO Ed Clark explains, "The great thing about our model is that if I put a bank branch on a corner in New York City, I know that five years later I will have more than 25 percent of the local business, because at some time in that five years someone will come by at 4:02 p.m. Their own bank branch will be closed; then they'll look across at our store, this beautiful store. There will be someone giving dog biscuits to somebody's dog. They'll walk in, and there's a greeter who is unbelievably friendly, and they'll say, 'So why am I banking across the street?'"

The final mystery is that we think donors who suddenly stop giving are acting rationally. Fundraisers look at the analysis and the database and cannot figure out how somebody so engaged and generous decided to stop giving, after all our fantastic work and the tons of calls and letters an organization sent. The point, again, is that we think of the "donor sapiens"—somebody very rational who makes a rational decision to stop their support. The reality, though, is that a donor's disaffection and attrition are not an isolated decision in a given time, but the sum of bad experiences (or no experiences) that the donor had with the organization.

A Bain & Company study found out that "customers have already been primed to leave by the time an alternative attractive offer arrives, so that any change in their lives can bring the decision to a head. The episodes that condition a customer to dislike his or her provider, and the actual decision to leave, can be years apart."[94] The other interesting insight is that there is a fine line between a customer who declares himself/herself to be "satisfied" and the moment they switch to a competitor. Because it is not what the customer says but what they experience. Therefore, it doesn't matter how many thank you notes, surveys and newsletters you send if the donor doesn't feel emotionally engaged.

When I decided to use my birthday to raise funds for charity: water there was a glitch in their system that prevented the acceptance of several credit cards. Having friends all over the world who wanted to contribute, I complained heavily to the organization. After several apology emails and the resolution of the problem, I received a handwritten card from them from New York. As you can see, it is not a generic "thank you" but a genuine acknowledgment and an apology with the phrase, "We think you rock!" that is, to this day, the best ever thing I've received from a charity!

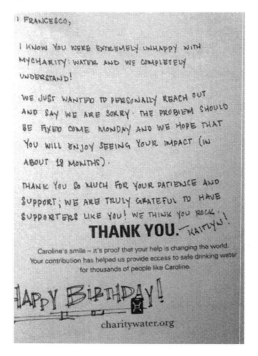

Fig. 8.74. Greeting card from charity: water.

94. http://www.bain.com/publications/articles/breaking-the-back-of-customer-churn.aspx

Mystery shopping in the fundraising world

One of the issues in our job, like in many other jobs or industries, is that we create processes and standards. We clearly need them to optimize our work, to plan resources and to be efficient and effective, especially when we have complex operations and huge numbers of donors and communications to handle.

The problem is that we become so addicted to the processes that often we believe they are the reality. So donors are "lapsed" or "active," and what we communicate is the "welcome pack" or the "upgrade call." There is nothing wrong with that—on the contrary they are great tools for being more targeted and personal.

However, the problem is that we forget these are just labels, and that a "regular donor"—who we created on the basis of his/her history in our database—does not exist in reality and his/her experience when dealing with us is completely different from what we would like, or imagine, it to be.

We all know about the importance of donor retention and loyalty. Who has not tried and tested, and has a great system in place online and offline to welcome and thank donors? And yet how many donors do we lose every day, week and year?

With a group of bright and experienced fundraisers from around the world—from Argentina to Germany, from Canada to the U.K. and Australia—at the 2013 International Fundraising Congress in Holland, we tried to do what millions of people do every day: make a donation to a nonprofit organization. Armed with real money, a phone and a laptop, these fundraisers tried to donate online, to call and to make a one-off donation or leave a legacy to the top ten nonprofits in several countries.

Here is summary of what they experienced during these calls or navigating the websites. I've attempted not to edit their accounts because I firmly believe in a fundamental principle: donors will forget what you said and what you did, but will never forget how you made them feel. And this how a fundraiser trying to walk in the donor's shoes feels. Just imagine, it's 5 p.m. on a normal day and you are about to make a donation to your favourite cause or organization. Here's what can happen:

We tried to leave a legacy...

"If you walked into a restaurant or a Bentley shop with $100,000 in cash you would be treated like royalty. And there is no way they would let you walk out with that money if they could help it. When you call a charity to talk about a legacy, that is potentially who you are. Yet our experience was very much as though we were an admin caller. No passion, no emotion,

131

no "thank you," and no discussion about the work of the organization. More like we were calling our bank. During the call I said that I was going to see my solicitor soon. It's now Thursday (over a week later) and I haven't yet received the information they promised, so in real life the likelihood is that that £100,000 (or £1,000, or £1,000,000) would now have gone somewhere else."

"The lady who picked up the phone was cold and unfriendly and said that at 5 p.m. she did not know who the right person to talk was, and that I had to call again the day after. It was hard to get any information from her—no call back offer, no need to give me any feeling of being important for the organization. Did they need legacies?"

"We rang and the person on the line was very informative but didn't once ask the name of the legator or the name of the caller. He also didn't ask for our contact details, despite us asking for his!"

"The animal welfare charity failed to mention animals or their welfare at any point during a conversation with a legacy prospect, focusing on meaningless jargon and an obvious desire to end the call and leave the office (well, it was almost 5 p.m.—which would explain why it had taken us three attempts before we managed to find anyone willing to talk to us about legacies)."

And we tried to make a donation...

"To this day I have not received an email receipt for my online gift."

"When I asked where our gift would go, one of the worst phrases I have ever heard was: Into the head office collection account!"

"The animal charity was so focused on the marketing of their adoption product they overlooked the experience for donors who just wanted to leave a simple cash gift—all the emotion, cause-related messaging and supporter care they lavished upon adopters was wholly missing from other donation processes."

"After searching and searching for where I can click to donate, I found the right button in between of thousands of links, and then I arrived to a pizza-like website. There was a big link "donate now," so, full of hope I clicked. The exact same site loaded again and again... I scrolled down and there was finally a wonderful little donation tool at the end of the site. And it works. My donation was done successfully after 15 minutes of hard work!"

But there is hope

"The contrast with the cash call we made is stark—friendly, passionate, and ready to go and find more information, all in return for a £10 donation. I wonder if this is about timing and feedback. Would you do more for £10 now or a possible £100,000 later? Rationally, you'd say the £100,000, but charities seem set up to pursue the £10."

"At the end of the conversation he asked about my friend, the reason why I want to donate to this particular charity. Did she get everything she needed from them? Could they send her more books? And would I please give my friend their number, so she could call them to make sure they are doing everything they can for her? My money was already being put to good use!"

"I found a telephone number for the legacy fundraiser on their site. I phoned it and was hugely surprised it was answered immediately. I felt like apologizing to them for being surprised—it was a great call, they did a great job."

And the winner is...

We know that emotions drive decisions. We know as fundraisers and we know because behavioural economics and neuroscience is increasingly producing evidence about it. And yet we focus all our efforts on the rational part of our communication: the processes, the targets, the calendar, the report.

- **Walk the talk.** Donate regularly to your organization, via phone, online and offline. You can learn so much about the real experience of a donor and you can immediately identify gaps and issues to resolve and improve it. As one of the participants said, "call your organization as a donor and find out where the gaps are to becoming a really donor-friendly and powered-by-service organization." And do the same with other organizations; you can learn and copy so many good things.
- **Make it personal and live.** We know people give to people, and we know the importance of a personalized donor service. So why do we have on our websites a number to call without a real person to pick up the phone? Or why should the call be like calling a bank or the tax office? It doesn't take

much to have a 24/7 real person, warm and passionate about our cause. If companies like Zappos invested most of their marketing budget on this to drive revenues, why shouldn't we?

- **How do you feel?** Finally, let's try to use the hard data and processes to support the emotional connection we want to create with donors, starting from a different point of view: How do we want to make them feel? Because it is not only the transaction or the demographics that make a donor engaged; it's the wow factor we can deliver in every interaction and experience.

Delivering happiness, or not?

Donors are not happy and we are not taking them seriously, according to Joe Saxton. We are not listening (whether they complain or they change address) and we fail to keep them as happy as they were when they first donated. Last year, I conducted a number of mystery calls to some Italian charities to understand the experience of donors. A summary can be watched here (https://www.youtube.com/watch?v=Sb_dumubzDg), and you don't need to know the language to understand. Apart from the long waiting time on the line and the ill-informed respondents about charity activities, and about what difference the donations can make, the overall experience for the donors has been dull and emotion-less. Examples of what donors said after the experience of calling their charity with a query include: "Lack of courtesy. She didn't know the programs and she is not passionate about the cause; she didn't engage with me at all." "He gave me comprehensive information about their programs but sounded very cold, and even when he thanked me it was like he was reading a script."

It's no surprise that we lose most of our first-time donors while the commercial sector retains most of their customers. One of the best examples is Zappos, an online shoe seller in the U.S. This company grew into a multi-billion-dollar company, starting without a marketing budget but relying only on customer satisfaction and referral through word of mouth. Zappos's vision is "Delivering Happiness" (a vision that could apply to many charities!) and is based on a few simple principles like "wowing customers" (they deliver shoes overnight for free and, in case they don't fit, you can return them for free within 365 days) and building open and honest relationships through communication, and are passionate and determined. Results: 75 percent of purchases are from returning customers, and repeat customers order more than 2.5 times every 12 months. Repeat customers also have higher average-order volumes, and year-over-year revenue has gone up by 30 percent. When I spoke with Zappos's Chief of Happiness (head of customer care) she explained that the key to their success is that each person on the customer care team—1,300 people for 25 million customers—has total autonomy both in terms of decisions and budget. When a customer experiences a problem, a delay in the delivery or has a complaint, anyone who picks up the call or reads the email can decide to do whatever it takes to make the customer happy (including sending flowers or a pizza, and staying on the phone for one hour or more), without supervisor approval. Can you imagine if our donor/supporter care team, our people in call centres or our face-to-face teams were empowered to make any decision they deem necessary to make donors happy—including spending money—without approval from managers or directors?

Do it like George Bailey!

Irrespective of Christmas, there is something we can use from the festive spirit. Everyone knows the movie *It's a Wonderful Life*, directed by Frank Capra, in which the angel Clarence shows George Bailey (played by James Stewart) how the world would look if he had not been born. This is called "counterfactual reflection" and strengthens the engagement of customers and employees. Researchers at Northwestern University and UC Berkeley found that having people visualize historical alternatives made them more engaged and committed with institutions and organizations. Jeff Brooks[95] argues that to improve engagement and loyalty we should show the donors what the world would look like without their giving. We can use the idea of a magic wand, or simply help them imagine a world without our charity or without our donors. An example from an Italian NGO called Emergency[96] shows in two minutes, through clever use of info-graphics, what the world would look like thanks to the donors and Emergency successes. No wonder Emergency received last year most of the tax declarations from donors. Or look at the way Amnesty International in Australia used one page of images and donors' quotes to show the world in 2012, or the superb American Red Cross campaign[97] in which people helped tell the story of how their lives changed thanks to Red Cross.

We need to recreate emotional connections with our donors and stop treating the donor care or support team as a cost or a simple newsletter. Our causes and

95. http://www.futurefundraisingnow.com/future-fundraising/2011/01/show-donors-the-world-without-their-giving.html
96. https://www.youtube.com/watch?v=4i2ih338e68
97. http://www.redcross.org/about-us/who-we-are/red-cross-stories

stories can trigger powerful emotions, but we fail to keep the same emotional connection with our donors after the first gift.

More important than the technologies or the fundraising models we use is the actual experience, and that a donor decides to stay with us because, as the poet Maya Angelou said, "I've learned that people will forget what you said, people will forget what you did, but people will never forget how you made them feel."

ADVICE AND PRACTICAL TOOLS

Emotions are the key also to a healthy, long-term and sustainable relationship with donors.

Customer attrition in the commercial world is lower than in the nonprofit sector.

The commercial world understands that emotionally satisfied customers are substantially more profitable compared to rationally satisfied or dissatisfied customers. We should invest in more emotional engagement with donors AFTER the donations, and not only in acquiring new donors and then sending institutional/transactional/rational communications.

You should donate regularly to your organization, via phone, online and offline. As one of the participants said, "Call your organization as a donor and find out where the gaps are to become a really donor-friendly, powered-by-service organization."

Invest in a personalized donor service, with a 24/7 "real person," and be warm and passionate about the cause.

Use data and processes to support the emotional connection we want to create with donors starting from a different point of view: How do we want to make them feel? Because it is not only the transaction or the demographics that make a donor engaged; it's the wow factor we can deliver in every interaction and experience.

Chapter 9

Til death do us part:
Emotions in legacies and bequests

Legacies can be the biggest source of fundraising and charitable income for many nonprofit organizations.

- In the U.K., legacies to charities represents £2 billion each year.
- In the U.S.A., legacies amounts to $19 billion a year.
- In Canada, legacies represent $1 billion a year.
- In Italy, it's estimated that between 2004 and 2020, legacies to non-profits will amount to €105 billion.

As Richard Radcliffe,[98] the worldwide expert on legacy fundraising, reminds us, each culture, religion and country has different will-making and legacy-giving traditions. In most developed countries, and in Anglo-Saxon countries, 45 percent – 50 percent of adults at any given time have a will in place. However, there are exceptions to the rule and in some parts of Europe, and, due to Napoleonic inheritance laws, there is little motivation to make a will because legally there are definitive rules concerning family inheritance. In France, for example, only about 5 percent of the adult population have a will.

However, while in certain cultures people start early in life to think about and prepare a will, in all cultures the strongest predictor of a charitable legacy is child-lessness. Without question, people without children are more inclined to leave a legacy.

How closely can the decision of leaving a part or everything of one's inheritance be related to emotions? Very closely.

Nobody has spent more of their life and career investigating the role of emotions and how the brain works in the process of making a will or leaving a legacy to charities than Russel N. James, Professor at Texas Tech University.[99]

The first interesting discovery is that when we are involved in the act of

---

98. http://radcliffeconsulting.org/
99. Russel N. James, *Inside the Mind of the Bequest Donor: A visual presentation of the neuroscience and psychology of effective planned giving communication*, CreateSpace Independent Publishing Platform, 2013.

decision making around a legacy there are two regions of the brain that are particularly active, more than others: the lingual gyrus and precuneus.

The lingual gyrus is part of the visual system, and damage to it can result in losing the ability to dream, while the precuneus has been called "the mind's eye," and is used in taking a third- person perspective on one's self.

In a study in which older adults were shown photographs from throughout their lives, precuneus and lingual gyrus activation occurred when they were able to vividly relive events in the photos, but not where scenes were only vaguely familiar.[100] In other studies, both regions were simultaneously activated by mentally "traveling back in time"[101] or recalling autobiographical personal events.[102]

This therefore suggests, according to James, that telling the life stories of donors who will live beyond their death through their legacy giving is a very powerful mechanism to engage donors to consider leaving a legacy to a nonprofit organization.

A second important element is that legacies to friends and family (vs. charitable legacies) more heavily involve brain regions of emotion (mid/posterior cingulate cortex; insula) and memory (hippocampus).

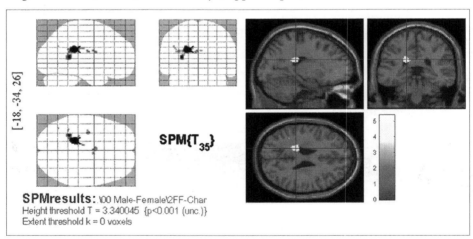

Fig. 9.75. Activation of precuneus and lingual gyrus in decision making on bequests.

100. Moscovitch, Morris, R.; Shayna Rosenbaum; Asaf Gilboa; Donna Rose Addis; Robyn Westmacott: "Functional neuroanatomy of remote episodic, semantic and spatial memory: A unified account based on multiple trace theory," *Journal of Anatomy*, July 2005, 207(1): 35–66.

101. Armelle Viard; Gael Chetelat; Karine Lebreton; Beatrice Desgranges; Brigitte Landeau; et al.: "Mental time travel into the past and the future in healthy aged adults: An fMRI study," *Brain and Cognition*, Elsevier, 2011, 75 (1), pages 1-9.

102. Denkova, E.; Botzung, A.; Scheiber, C.; Manning, L.: "2006 Implicit emotion during recollection of past events: A nonverbal fMRI study," *Brain Research*, 1078143–150.150.

This also suggests reminding donors of life story connections of friends/family with the charity/cause and providing tribute legacy opportunities. In a 2014 survey cited by James, one in four people polled increased their intention to leave a charitable bequest when given the option to honour a friend or family member by making a memorial gift to charity in their last will and testament. In addition, giving examples of past history and connections to the past lives of potential donors can substantially increase the number of people deciding to leave a legacy to a charity.

Another important element is that the main obstacle to leaving a legacy—the simple avoidance of talking about a legacy because it is a reminder of our own death. In fact, the first stage of defense to death reminders is avoidance. James therefore suggested that since the topic of legacies—a reminder of death—is subconsciously aversive, we need to combine (or mask) the idea of leaving a legacy with more attractive topics to sidestep the initial avoidance response. For instance, using stories about the work of the nonprofit and focusing on the support of legacy donors who make it happen can help overcome this first stage of defense.

The second stage of defense to death reminders that naturally happens when we talk about the possibility of leaving a legacy is to seek symbolic immortality by supporting one's "in-group" community. This means that the death reminder increases the desire for fame and the perception of one's past significance (Landau, Greenberg, & Sullivan, 2009[103]).

This suggests, according to James, that when we promote the opportunity to leave a legacy to a charity we should provide also the idea that a legacy is connected with permanence. Permanence is psychologically attractive because it is something reflecting a sort of autobiographical heroism, through the person's life story (community and values). In previous surveys, among people expressing a difference in preference, more than half wanted permanence for their legacy than for current gifts. Between the options of the legacy gift going to "an immediate expenditure of all funds to advance the cause of the charity" and "the establishment of a permanent fund generating perpetual income to advance the cause of the charity forever," the latter was much more preferred. This specific process can be further promoted through scholarships, lectureships, annual performances, perpetual child sponsorship, perpetual rescued pet sponsorship, a memorial wall of heroes, etc., which includes the names of legacy donors.

How can neuroscience help in legacy fundraising by using emotions more effectively? At UNICEF in Italy, we developed a new legacy campaign doing just that.

---

103. Landau, Greenberg, & Sullivan, *Toward Understanding the Fame Game: The Effect of Mortality Salience on the Appeal of Fame, Self and Identity*, 9: 1–18, 2010.

We had an established program that worked quite well but it was flat over the years in terms of requests for information and wills. This is due to the changing media landscape (direct mail is more expensive, for instance) as well changing demographics. We knew, however, from an analysis of the past 10 years, that our target was clearly over 65 years old and without children. Our dilemma was how to reach and maximize the potential for legacies (Italy has one of the highest populations of elderly people); meanwhile, we were facing the challenge of the first-stage of defense to death reminders: avoidance.

So we developed a strategy with a central focus on TV through 30- and 60-second videos. We produced two videos and then tested them in the laboratory to see if they were able to ignite emotions and therefore drive people to consider leaving a legacy to UNICEF.

The first spot was a relatively classic Direct Response Television (DRTV) spot with a beginning based on nostalgia, with images of childhood and a voice-over saying, "When you were sad, who comforted you?"; "When you were hungry, who fed you?" It then showed images of children in difficult situations, saying that today there are millions of children who need the same help that you received when you were a child.

The second spot used as a main creative hook the photo of a real legacy donor that is passed through the hands of children in various situations and places, with the voiceover saying, "One day, somebody will talk about you and they will tell why you decided to leave a legacy...so that when are you no longer on this planet, you will be here for them again and again."

With the Brainlab of IULM, a university in Milan, we tested the two spots to identify which was working better in terms of arousal of emotion and engagement. The panel of donors, over 65, male and female, with children and with no children, were shown the two spots while a number of biometric inputs were gathered through ECG, eye tracker and skin conductance as well as facial reading.

The test results were really interesting. First of all, we noticed that the second spot worked much better than the first one in terms of engagement and emotional activation. As you can see from the two charts, which summarize all the biometric input frame by frame, the second spot has in fact two major peaks of arousal at two crucial moments: 1. When the spot says, "because when you are no longer here on this earth" (therefore making a direct reference to death but with the sweetest visual moment—when a child kisses the photo of the donor), and 2. At the very crucial moment of the call to action, "if you want to create a legacy, call this number." The first spot, in contrast, had the lowest point of arousal at the call-to-action moment, a clear signal that the audience is not engaged.

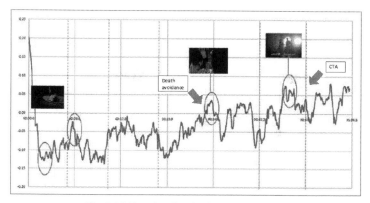

Fig. 9.76. Emotional activation on spot no. 2.

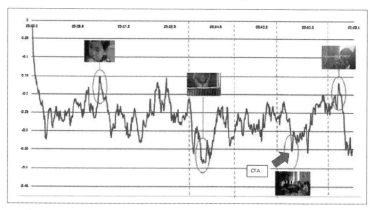

Fig. 9.77. Emotional activation on spot no. 1.

The second important element in terms of attention is that the eye-tracking revealed that the attention of the audience in the second spot is all about the photo and the face of the donor, an indication that the idea of putting the donor at the centre of the message—with its reference to symbolic immortality as mentioned before—works very well.

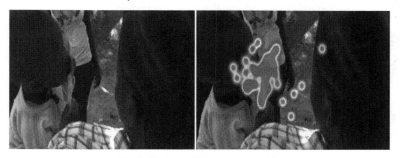

Fig. 9.78. Eye tracking on spot no. 2.

Finally, the second spot works even better among those potential donors without children, another important confirmation that the message is perfectly emotionally targeted for our identified audience.

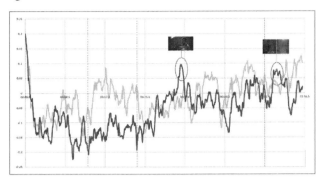

Fig. 9.79. Emotional engagement on spot no. 2.

ADVICE AND PRACTICAL TOOLS

Legacies can be the biggest source of income for many nonprofit organizations. Emotions are crucial in the process of making a will or leaving a legacy to charities.

Two regions of the brain that are particularly active, more than others: the lingual gyrus and precuneus. This suggests that telling the life stories of donors who will live beyond their death through their legacy giving is a very powerful mechanism to engage donors.

Legacies to friends and family more heavily involve the brain regions of emotion (mid/posterior cingulate cortex; insula) and memory (hippocampus). This also suggests that reminding donors of the life-story connections of friends/family with the charity/cause provides tribute legacy opportunities.

Since talking of legacies is subconsciously an aversive topic, we need to combine (or mask) the idea of leaving a legacy with more attractive topics to sidestep the initial avoidance response, using stories. When we promote the opportunity to leave a legacy to a charity we should also promote the idea that a legacy is connected with permanence.

PART THREE

It's all over your face: How to recognize emotions during interaction with donors and supporters

Let's not forget that the little emotions
are the great captains of our lives,
and we obey them without realizing it.

—Vincent van Gogh

INTRODUCTION

In the first part of this book we have seen how emotions guide our decisions, especially when we decide to donate to an organization or to a social cause. Emotions that stimulate the decision-making process take place on a subconscious level, without us realizing it. Therefore, if emotions are unconscious, how do we know if they are active or not, and which of them can lead to an action or a reaction?

In Part Three, we will discover how marketing and neuroscience, in particular the work of Paul Ekman and through the use of sophisticated techniques such as FACS (Facial Action Coding System), have come to a better understanding of the emotional response to campaigns and advertising messages and how this is also crucial for fundraising.

In Chapter 10, after a brief overview of the main technology available for the study of emotions, we will focus on facial reading as the main instrument to understanding whether what we are saying or showing through our appeals are making their way through to the emotions of a donor.

In Chapter 11, we will briefly discuss other elements (voice, gestures, etc.) that, although less important than the face, can help us understand better and to interact with the emotions of our potential and current donors.

Chapter 10

Let's face it:
Emotions and micro-facial
expressions

Developments in neuroscience in recent years have proven that people are intuitive in their decisions and decide on actions based on sensory and emotional stimuli. Market research, however, has developed an approach based on asking consumers via questionnaires and focus groups if and how much they like a particular ad, and whether they are willing to buy a product. The assumption has been that if somebody declares they prefer certain brands or remember a product or an advertising campaign, this will result in a purchase behaviour (or in a donation).

However, as Daniel Kahneman said, 95 percent of what we think happens at an unconscious level and sensory impressions and their emotional responses are anchored in some parts of the brain whose origins date back hundreds of millions of years. The sensory brain (also called reptilian) and the emotional brain (mammalian) work together. The rational brain (or that of the human) is considerably more recent, in evolutionary terms, since it developed about 100,000 years ago.

Traditional market research usually invites participants to give marks to specific questions or statements—for example, "What motivates you to donate: Here's a list from 1 to 10…". This is an invitation to participants to provide rational answers or intellectual arguments that often do not reveal the true motivations behind certain actions or behaviour. As J.P. Morgan said, "A man always has two reasons for doing anything: a good reason and the real reasons." The good reasons are the rational justification to a behaviour, and the real reasons are the behaviour itself. Neuroscience and behavioural economics suggest that the real reasons are often found in what people cannot or will not say. Consider the mistake often made in exit polls: voters are often ashamed to say for whom they truly voted.

However, there are now five main types of research techniques that can help us to identify the real emotions at work: the electroencephalogram (EEG), magnetic resonance imaging (fMRI), eye tracking, skin conductance and facial micro expressions coding (FAACS).[104]

These five main technologies are often combined with the collection of other sensory stimuli like the heartbeat, and proper neuro-marketing research and can be used with the combination of 25 different data sets or more per second, during which a subject is looking at a video or a piece of advertising. This type of research will be much more effective in telling us the true picture.

The electroencephalogram (EEG). Used by many neuroscientists and neuro-marketing researchers like Sands Research (http://www.sandsresearch.com/), which since 2008 has analysed reactions to commercials during the Super Bowl (the biggest TV event in terms of audience in the U.S.). This instrument works with the attachment of electrodes to the scalp through a sort of "headphone," and is used to monitor the electrical activity of the brain. Recognized scientifically as a means to capture what occurs in the brain, second by second, the EEG does not have the precision of other sensorial techniques. In fact, in mammals the emotional part is "hidden" in the deep part of the brain within the skull and is therefore relatively inaccessible to the readings of the electrodes.

Functional magnetic resonance imaging (fMRI). This has led to discoveries of relatively new areas for neuroscience and neuro-marketing. The basic goal of neuro-marketing is to get a deeper understanding of the neural mechanisms underlying the behaviour of the consumer, through a better understanding of consumers' feelings about the products and the reasons for purchase. MRI observes the changes in blood flow that accompany a specific neural activity in different parts of the brain and associate the areas that "light up" with particular behaviours. Studies using magnetic resonance imaging typically have a limited sample size because of the cost. In addition, the complexity of the brain (10 billion neurons), the delay in the photograph of the peaks of blood flow and the invasiveness of the technology limit the use of this tool in market research.

Eye tracking. The eye tracker is a technology that accurately determines where the eyes are focusing during a visual stimulation. When looking at something, the eyes move at least three times per second. Any movement (called saccadic movement) takes about a 10th of a second, while the "stops," or fixations, last from 2/10ths to 4/10ths of a second. During the saccadic movements, the view is completely blurred and you are able to define what fades before the eyes of the person. It is only during the fixations that people are able to define with

---

104. Dan Hill and Aron Levin, "Applying facial coding to ad testing. On the face of it", in QUIRCK's, March 2013, http://www.quirks.com/articles/2013/20130309.aspx

precision the reality they are observing. By recording both saccadic movements and fixations the eye tracker is then able to identify the elements that have captured the attention of the person (fixations) and the exploration (saccades). The principle behind eye-tracking research is the so-called eye-mind assumption that what a person is looking also reflects what we are thinking.

Skin conductance. The galvanic skin response depends on the activity of the sweat glands (under the control of the nervous system), which do not respond to the individual's conscious control. The sweat contains a conductive salt solution, which determines an increase of the capacity of the skin to conduct electrical current ("skin conductance"). This variation is detected through a device placed on the fingers or on the palms. A conductivity increase, due to an increased production of sweat, is attributable to a stronger activation of sweat glands controlled by the nervous system through the hypothalamus and is an index of arousal (activation).

Facial micro expressions. Darwin was the first scientist to take emotions seriously (as a survival mechanism), and also the first to realize that the face reflects and communicates the most our emotions. This is due to three main reasons:

- Universality—the way we feel emotions is hard wired in our brain and goes beyond factors such as gender, age, race and culture to the point that even a person born blind has the same emotional arousal those with full vision.
- Spontaneity—the face is the only part of our body where muscles are attached directly to the skin, allowing the transmission of data in real time via a brain-face connection through the nerves of facial muscles right under the ear.
- Abundance—human beings have more facial muscles than any other species on the planet.

A century later, Darwin's initial findings were consolidated into the Facial Action Coding System (FACS) by Paul Ekman and Wally Freisen. The classification is based on the recognition of facial muscle movements (called unity of action) corresponding to the seven basic emotions: happiness, surprise, sadness, fear, anger, disgust and contempt.[105] This system provides a formidable tool for the identification and quantification of emotional response without the use of invasive techniques like sensors or magnetic resonance.

Before getting into the specific analysis of the six emotions through the

---

105. With respect to Ekman's classification we simplified unifed contempt and disgust as very similar in expression.

analysis of micro-facial expressions, let's try to understand better why the face is more important than body language and more important than the words we are saying. Much of this chapter, and much of this book, is due to the work of Dan Hill, a pioneer in coding micro-facial expressions and emotions in marketing.

According to Dan Hill,[106] there are six reasons for paying attention to the face in marketing and fundraising.

1. Reading and recognizing facial expressions is such a vital aspect for the survival of humans that there is a specific part of the brain dedicated to analyzing the face. This area is called the fusiform face area (FFA), and is located near the visual part of the brain, which means that an active face attracts an important part of the brain and when a face moves (e.g. when smiling or crying), our brain notices a movement and we are inclined to pay attention to that movement.

2. The FFA is a very sophisticated tool. For example, in the flipped image of the Mona Lisa, at first we did not notice any difference between the two images, but when the images are inverted, we realize that they have different expressions. This is because when we look at the image upside down our brain reads the inverted image as an object. FFA is activated only when we realize that we are looking at a face. This means that using faces in communication increases our chances of drawing attention and engaging an audience.

Fig. 10.80.

3. According to a study cited by Hill, macaques, which are genetically almost identical to us, have 182 brain cells that respond to faces or heads and none of them respond not to unanimated objects. Of these cells, 63

---

106. Dan Hill, *Emotionomics: Leveraging emotions for business success*, Revised edition, Kogan Page, 2008; Dan Hill, *About Face: The secrets of emotionally effective advertising*, Kogan Page, 2010.

percent are sensitive to the orientation of the head, and half of these are geared toward the face. In several experiments, when a face turns away, this corresponds to a decrease of attention and emotion on the part of who is looking. The so-called "money shot" in Direct Response Television (DRTV)—the final frame when a child or animal looks into the camera and the voice says "call now"—is an example of this principle.

4. The ability to read facial expressions is a function carried out principally by the right hemisphere of the brain, where the emotional part is located. Looking at other individuals engages us emotionally. Since this part of the brain is oriented more toward the emotions and that the reactions in our body are physically opposite to those suggested by the brain, the left part of our face is normally more expressive than the right part, especially when it comes to negative expressions.

5. Our facial expressions are contagious. As we saw in the first chapter, thanks to mirror neurons, we tend to feel what another person feels and shows on his/her face.

6. Facial expressions are stored in neural circuits in what are called facial recognition units (FRU). It is estimated that we can remember up to 10,000 faces. Whenever we see a new face our brain does a quick search in the archive to look for a corresponding image. In our memories, the faces are recorded thanks to the repetition. There are so-called FRU "hot" as in the case of a stranger who reminds us of someone we were in love with and that triggers a strong emotional response. The use of famous people or celebrities can help in our fundraising because the emotional memory (the hippocampus) is activated when we recognize a famous face. But not necessarily. According to research by Hill, some particularly emotional faces of unknown actors can trigger greater emotional response than those of famous people. *For those who are interested in learning more about this technique, and want to be certified as a face reader and analyst using the FACS system, you can go to Paul Ekman's site (https://www.paulekman.com/content/what-facs).*

Now let's see now how we can identify and recognize the six key emotions through reading or decoding micro-facial expressions.

Emotionmeter©

JOY	AMAZEMENT	RAGE	LOATHING	GRIEF	TERROR
HAPPINESS	SURPRISE	ANGER	DISGUST	SADNESS	FEAR
Satisfaction	Curiosity	Annoyance	Boredom	Pensiveness	Worry

HIGH INTENSITY EMOTIONS/low intensity emotions
Adapted from Hill and Ekman

Fig. 10.81. States of emotional intensity, according to Ekman and The Emotionmeter©.

It is also necessary to point out that in the following pages, the expressions shown in the photos are exaggerated and emphasized, to make it clear to readers which parts they need to observe.

Many of the expressions represented in the photos are normally seen in a much less marked way and, above all, they take place at a very rapid rate (less than a second). This is why the analysis of facial expressions needs the skills of a professional or the use of videos that allow you to observe micro-expressions frame by frame. Furthermore, as already explained, emotions are manifested in combinations and different mixes so it is really very difficult, without proper preparation and practice, to distinguish one from another.

SADNESS

Fig. 10.82.

It is one of the strongest emotions. It typically occurs between birth and the first three months of life. In the case of sadness, the following are the key signs to observe on the face:

- The eyebrows are lowered, but the inner ends point upwards.
- The muscle that raises the inner corners of the eyebrows creates the appearance of wrinkles on the forehead. When this does not happen, the expression indicates a slight sadness (melancholy), or an attempt to mitigate a deeper feeling. Sadness is deeper when the lower lid is lifted. The gaze is turned down, especially when you are sad and feelings are mixed with shame or guilt.
- The movement of the eyebrows is lowering the upper eyelids and the same muscles make the eyelids under the eyes thin.
- The corners of the mouth are lowered, while the upper lip is pushed upwards and forms wrinkles on the chin, which is pushed upwards.
- The cheeks are raised and produce a kind of gap from the sides of the nostrils to the corners of the mouth.
- A lower or higher level of intensity of sadness can be indicated by the lower involvement of the facial areas.

On one extreme level, tears in the corners of the eyes and trembling of the lips can appear, indicating a higher level of sadness, and on the other extreme a face that's completely expressionless—as if you have the loss of muscle tone of the face —can indicate a lower level of sadness.

ANGER

Fig. 10.83

Anger normally appears on the face of a baby between three and seven months of life. An angry face shrinks and becomes more focused and intense.

- The upper and lower eyelids are stretched and tend to huddle together. The eyes are partially covered. When the eyes are open anger is mild, while when the eyes are closed or tightened anger is more intense.

- The eyebrows are lowered and converge. Darwin defined these muscles as "the difficulty muscles" because every difficulty makes us frown.
- The lips are joined. This is a very difficult symptom to hide if you are really angry. The upper lip is raised and the lower one is lowered. Pursed lips indicate that the subject is about to attack physically or verbally, or is taking action to control anger, while an open mouth signals somebody is about to cry.

SURPRISE

Fig. 10.84.

The ability to show surprise appears right from birth. As mentioned, surprise is neither negative nor positive. Because we are faced with a mystery, we do not know whether to expect pleasure or pain and we remain paralyzed. When we are surprised our face widens at top and bottom, right and left, and is similar to the expression we have when we are afraid. Surprise is an emotion that very rapidly leaves room for other emotions.

- The upper eyelids are raised (but if they are raised too much, it more likely means that we are afraid).
- The eyebrows are raised and the eyes are wide open.
- The jaw relaxes and remains down like an "open mouth" (not always in an obvious way).
- The sclera, or the white part of the eye over the iris, is visible.

FEAR

Fig. 10.85.

This is the strongest emotion, for evolutionary reasons. The capacity to show this emotion appears between five and nine months of life.

Fear widens your face and, in extreme cases, makes your face tremulous. Often surprise and fear are associated, because what generates fear is also frequently unexpected.

- The eyebrows are raised and closer, but unlike surprise, they are less curved.
- Wrinkles appear, like in surprise, but do not take up the whole front.
- The eyes are dilated with the lower lid taut.
- The lips are ironed back and the mouth is open. If the mouth looks similar to fear and the rest of the face is neutral, this indicates, rather, anxiety and worry.

DISGUST

Fig. 10.86.

Disgust shows that we want to distance ourselves from something dangerous or that we do not like. It is manifested by the nose and lips being curled, meaning that something or someone has a bad smell or taste. This emotion first occurs between birth and three months of age.

- The upper lip is raised and the lower one is slightly pushed forward.
- The cheeks are raised, and this produces a change in the lower eyelid, shrinking the eye and creating wrinkles immediately below.
- The nose curls.
- The lower eyelids are raised and eyebrows are lowered.

HAPPINESS

Fig. 10.87.

As we have seen this is the only positive emotion of the six key emotions. This is because, from an evolutionary point of view, happiness is not essential for survival. This emotion is nevertheless present in infants from birth. The expression of happiness is characterized by signs in the lower part of the face and eyelids, while the area of the forehead and eyebrows are not necessarily involved.

- A smile includes an open mouth that shows upper teeth or both upper and lower teeth.
- Wrinkles depart from the nose and arrive at the corners of the mouth, stretching the corners of the mouth.
- The skin under the lower eyelid lifts forming the so-called "crow's feet."
- The cheeks are raised to narrow the eyes.

These are the main signs of a genuine smile (or "the Duchenne smile," which Ekman named after the French doctor who helped in his research). A genuine smile that indicates true happiness is impossible to counterfeit or fake.

However, there is a different kind of smile...

SOCIAL SMILE

Fig. 10.88.

Human beings have the unique ability to manipulate the muscles around the mouth but not around the eyes. This is why the smile of circumstance, which develops in the first three months of life, is the only one that does not denote an emotion but can be confused with a smile indicating happiness. In the social smile:

- The face becomes more round, the sides of the mouth tend to rise and cheeks move up.
- There is, however, no activity around the eyes to indicate the presence of a real smile.

What, then, are these clues of, and how can they can be useful in the practice of fundraising?

1. First, in a face-to-face meeting with donors, facial analysis can help to

better focus on the speaker, paying attention to his/her emotions and signaling if we are exciting our interlocutor and if he/she is ready to act with a donation. Their face will also guide us to understand what mix of emotions he or she is more sensitive to.

2. Secondly, facial readings will help to test the effectiveness of our appeals in various media like a mailing, a TV commercial or a website. Showing options for a campaign to a group of existing and potential donors can help to understand whether they work and which emotions we are activating. As we have seen in the case of UNICEF's legacy campaign, the analysis supported the choice of which TV spot worked best among the two proposed (the one able to elicit arousal in the crucial moments—when the voiceover says, "you will no longer be here" and "call this number to create a legacy"). Analysis of emotions through micro facial expressions can help us to understand if messages capture the attention of the audience, and what mix of emotions works best.

3. Finally, especially in a world where social media has a great capacity to convey messages and images, analysis of facial micro-expressions can help to have a more focused and consistent message for our causes and missions, avoiding the assumptions that certain words, statistical numbers, slogans, programs, etc., are shared by our supporters.

It must not be forgotten, however, that the analysis of facial micro expressions is a very sophisticated technique and requires the use of technologies and experts (as in the case of Sensory Logic or Sands Research) to analyze a combination of inputs and biometrical and behavioural data sets.

Chapter 11

The other parts of the body, and words

When we interact with other people, we remember and pay attention first to their face and their expression (55 percent), then to their tone of voice (38 percent) and only minimally to the words they say (7 percent).

Fig 11.89.

This is because our brain is programmed to pay attention and take action according to other people's faces rather than to their gestures. Dan Hill, having analyzed 20 years of facial coding in response to television commercials, shows how this is important:

- A close up of a person generates an emotional response 20 percent higher than images of groups or crowds;
- A person who is moving vs. one who is standing and speaking generates a greater emotional impact and response.

In a study by Deborah Small and Nicole Verrochi, fundraising appeals using sad faces generated more response than a neutral or happy face. Therefore, the face is the main vehicle for an emotionraising success. Among other things, one of the advantages of the analysis of facial micro-expressions is that they are universal and not dependent on cultural and geographical influences.

In this chapter we briefly look at the other components, like gestures or body language and words.

Voice

We have already seen in the first part of the book how voice is an important element of emotionraising. Dan Hill, who measured the emotional response to some radio spots, explains how the tone of voice generates various types of response:

a) People are about 24 percent more excited when listening to a message at a higher volume (this is why during commercial breaks, volume is higher).

b) A low tone of voice works best because it is associated with competence and authority.

c) Research indicates that those who speak more quickly have more influence on the listening audience.

d) Pauses guarantee the variability, and serve to reinforce curiosity and the element of surprise.

Tone of voice and rhythm are interesting not only in canvassing or street fundraising, but also in communication via telephone (telemarketing) and even when donors or potential donors call our offices for information or assistance in making a donation or a bequest.

Dan Hill gave a useful chart to identify how various types of tone, rhythm, scale and composition are linked to a specific emotion.

	FEAR	ANGER	SADNESS	HAPPINESS	DISGUST
Tone of voice	HIGH	HIGH	LOW	HIGH	LOW
Rhythm	FAST	INTERRUPT	SLOW	MIXED	SLOW
Extension	WIDE	WIDE	NARROW	WIDE	WIDE
Articulation of words	PRECISE	INTENSE	BABBLE	NORMAL	NORMAL

Fig 10.90.

The body

Body language and the signals that our body sends when we assume a posture or make a gesture can be a useful indicator for understanding the emotions or barriers that our interlocutors are trying to put forward.

The study of movements and body language is guided by a discipline called kinesiology, a discipline that studies human motility. Etymology refers to the Greek word "kinesis" meaning movement and "logos" meaning study. Applications of kinesiology to human health include biomechanics and orthopedics; strength and conditioning; sports psychology; methods of rehabilitation, such as physical and occupational therapy; and sport and exercise.

Physical expressions such as gesture or posture can reveal a lot about a person. For example, gestures can emphasize a point, or send a message, while a posture can reveal boredom or great interest, and a touch can convey encouragement or caution.

One of the powerful signs of body language is when a person crosses his arms over his chest. This may indicate that a person is putting up an unconscious barrier between himself and others. When the overall situation is amicable, it can indicate that a person is involved deeply in the discussion, but in a confrontational situation, it means that a person is expressing opposition or refusal. Reading of micro-facial expressions (like anger) can help to better understand what emotions are at work.

Fig. 10.91. Cezanne, "Man with crossed arms".

A second aspect is visual contact. A concentrated look at the speaker can indicate that a person is listening carefully to what the speaker is saying but it can also mean that he/she does not trust the speaker enough. Lack of eye contact can also indicate negativity, although it should be noted that eye contact can also be a secondary and misleading gesture because cultural norms vary widely. For example, in some countries or cultures staring at someone can be seen as a violation of intimacy and a lack of respect.

Other interesting clues (correlated with facial expressions) were also used in the television series *Lie to Me*, and are:

- Closure or clenching of your fist or fists: Strongly gripping an object or tightening a fist may indicate anger and aggression.
- Turning the ring on your finger: Playing with a ring, necklace or bracelet can have a sexual meaning, but more often is a pleasant involvement signal.
- Tapping your finger on your wrist or on your other hand: This can show impatience.
- Switching hands symmetrically on the temples: A hand that moves along the top of the head can be a form of self-reassurance.
- Closing your fingers, clawing your forearm: This indicates an attempt of manipulating or tricking someone.
- Passing your hand across your forehead and hair: This shows that somebody is considering a certain situation.

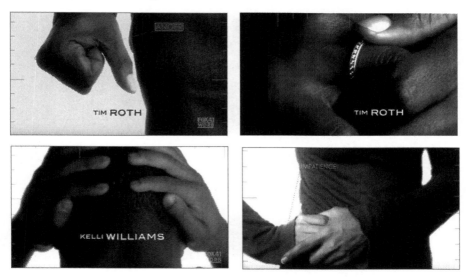

Fig. 10.92. Body gestures as used in the TV show Lie To Me.

In general, taking similar body positions or repeating the same gestures of the interlocutor can help in generating a certain empathy. This is what is called "mirroring" and "matching" but it should be used with caution to avoid giving the impression that we are making fun of our interlocutors.

ADVICE AND PRACTICAL TOOLS

If emotions guide our decisions—including the act of giving—and they are active in a subconscious part of our brain, how we can see when they are on?

For far too long market research concentrated only on methodologies and tools using the rational part of the brain (questionnaires, focus groups, etc.). Neuroscience now offers us the possibility of knowing what happens in our brains, to understand what we feel, not just what we think. While the EEG and MRI are powerful technologies, they have the disadvantage of not fully grasping the "hidden" part of the brain where emotions are activated, and they can be expensive and invasive techniques.

The analysis of facial micro-expressions (FACS) developed by Paul Ekman provides a powerful tool for understanding the emotions of our donors. Through the identification of specific facial signals we can understand if our appeals, our speech and our campaigns are generating an emotional involvement and therefore are activating the possibility of a donation.

The analysis of other specific signals provided by the tone and pace of voice and by body language can help to complement and corroborate the analysis of micro-facial expressions, but the face is still a more powerful tool for understanding if emotions are at stake in our fundraising.

PART FOUR

The good reasons
and the real reasons:
A conversation with Dan Hill
on emotions and fundraising

INTRODUCTION

Reading faces comes naturally for Dan Hill, a recognized authority on the role of emotions in consumer and employee behaviour. As a young boy living in Italy, he began using facial expressions to help navigate an unfamiliar setting. Today he runs Sensory Logic, Inc., a scientific insights firm that analyzes consumers' facial expressions to help companies better navigate their' emotionally-driven decision making process. This ability to capture and quantify marketplace insights "hidden" in plain sight is why Sensory Logic has helped over 35 percent of the world's top 100 marketers. It's also made Dan a frequent speaker at business conventions around the world. Press coverage of Sensory Logic and its methods include articles in The New York Times, USA Today, The Wall Street Journal, Advertising Age, TIME.com, Fast Company, Entrepreneur, LA Times, Bloomberg, and others. Dan has appeared on CNN, FOX, ESPN, CNN, NBC's "The Today Show," NPR's Marketplace and MSNBC. Dan received his Ph.D. from Rutgers University following study at Brown University, Oxford University, and St. Olaf College. Dan lives with his wife, Karen Bernthal, in St. Paul, Minnesota. If you are interested in Dan's work you can see more of his work and contact at www. sensorylogic.com

Q. What are the stronger emotions in driving decisions, especially in philanthropic giving?

A. I can't pretend to be an expert in emotional impulses related to philanthropic giving. The closest I've come to date to applying facial coding, and emotional analysis in general, to the nonprofit realm as a full-blown project is a recent project on childhood obesity for a branch of the U.S. government. But in terms of which emotions drive decisions, and what kind of behaviour they elicit, I could after 14 years of applied knowledge write yet another book—if I only had the time!

Let me offer a few observations, at least.

The brain's emotional "hot button," the amygdala, is oriented most of all to fear. That makes sense. After all, as a species human beings' first goal is survival. Fear, and the defend impulse that goes with it, is almost surely the strongest emotion that drives decisions. We want to defend ourselves, our family members, resources like food, water and shelter that keep us alive, and finally most of us also want to defend our beliefs or value system, which keep us spiritually alive. Only in regards to beliefs does philanthropic giving have much hope of enlisting fear on behalf of its fundraising efforts. After all, in other ways fear is a very selfish emotion, all about alert/danger/freeze. It doesn't move generosity forward very readily.

Happiness makes us relaxed and imaginative but also inattentive to the details (like writing that fundraising cheque!). So count it out. Much better is its opposite, sadness, which slows us down, makes us pay attention to the details, is in response to a sense of longing, of being forlorn, isolated, and at its most intense, without hope. Don't invoke sadness to the degree of "without hope" and it can really aid the cause of philanthropy giving. A pharmaceutical study we did in which each print ad sought to leverage a different emotion shows that sadness can be really potent in motivating people so that they can restore a feeling of happiness. Think of the poignancy of Eugenio Montale's poem about a Jewish lover lost to him during the rise of Fascism: "Life which had seemed so vast / is a tinier thing than your handkerchief."

Q. How to avoid the risk to be over-emotional and "block" a decision or cause rejection?

A. A cornered animal fights or flees. Any attempt in philanthropic giving to be too forceful—inspiring profound guilt, rage, sadness, whatever—is likely to fail. People like to buy but they don't like to be sold to. Nobody wants to feel like they're "prey." That's why I always favour the image or other visual to do the selling. Words are easily too pushy, but an image that invites the eye and is readily understood without forcing a conclusion is best. As the great 19th century American poet Emily Dickinson wrote, "Tell the truth but tell it slant, lest everyone go blind." A hard-edged, straight-on message will more likely than not inspire frustration, because one of the causes of frustration is a sense of wanting to be in control of your own life. The message that tells me what to do means that, if I follow it, I won't be in control of my own life.

Q. What are the mechanisms that control the emotions in regards to the decision to write a cheque, call a number, among other means of fundraising?

A. Boy, you're asking me to be the da Vinci of emotions! What a tough question! To attempt an answer, let's go back to Latin because emotion and motivation have the same root word in Latin, movere, to move or make something happen. That's what you're after with this question: How can I get the person taking in my request to donate monies, to actually take action. Besides the instinct to defend, the other four core motivations outlined by a pair of Harvard University professors are to bond (with others, or products, sensory perceptions, etc.); to acquire (possessions, rank, privileges, etc.); or to learn (self-discovery, knowledge, problem-solving, etc.). Different people will tend to exhibit certain of the seven core emotions more readily, and to orient also more readily to one of these core motivations. It's useful to figure out which. (Indeed, I have U.S. patents granted and filed that deal with this very topic.) For instance, a person given to the learning motivation is, I believe, more likely to respond to philanthropic pictures that utilize surprise because surprise as an emotion is all about being alert. With surprise, the eyes go wide (to take in more information) and the mouth falls open (to keep us from talking, and failing to notice the world around us). If fear goes with defend, then other fairly reasonable assumptions are that disgust (rejection) also goes with defend, anger (wanting control) goes with acquire, happiness and sadness go with bonding, and contempt goes against bonding, learning, but with acquiring and defending your view that you're superior to something or somebody else.

Now, see how well I've given an answer while dodging your impossible question?

Q. Are there simpler/cheaper methods of applying emotional measurement to gauge the effectiveness of fundraising techniques?

A. Certainly: track which work best in raising monies! But not to be glib, facial coding is certainly much more do-able than fMRI brain scans. Everybody's a facial coder; it's just that some people like myself are trained to be still better. Trust your instincts. Anger tightens the face. Sadness makes it droop. Disgust makes the nose wrinkle, the upper lip curl—as in bad taste, bad smell. Boredom by the way is a low-grade version of disgust, as in no taste at all (a sin in the Disneyfied world of today). Everyone can recognize a smile—or can they? In truth, a real smile makes the muscle around the eye relax and brings a twinkle to the eye. Almost nobody can fake it well. But social smiles that involve just the mouth involve endless degrees of deception. Never forget the opening line of Francis Bacon's great 17th century essay, "Of Truth," which opens: "'What is truth?' said jesting Pilate, and would not stay for an answer."

Q. How can facial coding, body language and voice be used during face to face interactions to influence a donor?

A. Let's start with ground truth: People are not truth machines. Essentially, we want to feel good about ourselves (pleasure) and to accrue allies (survival). Whatever his faults, Freud wasn't a dummy. Never forget the pleasure principle; in other words, make the donor feel good about him or herself because happiness makes people more expansive, more free-thinking, and also more careless (with their money). Don't flatter so as to put the person on guard. But you can invite them in to brainstorm on how the monies could be best used, and that kind of thing. A smile opens the door to acceptance, and a degree of your own smiling is good—if subtly done—as emotions are contagious. Even more important is to recognize that negative emotions, while often fleetingly shown, are disaster speed bumps that will slow down the transaction of monies to your cause. Notice the body pulling back, the voice going tight, or a smirk, and you're in trouble. Suck the poison out of the conversation if you can when such a signal indicates the presence of danger, and proceed where the other party verbally walks first.

Q. What are examples of emotional successes in business marketing?

A. My favourite remains the Michelin baby-inside-a-tire campaign that ran for years. It's brilliant. First, you take away the car because the car is far sexier than a dirty, black tire. Next, you take the single most vulnerable and precious human cargo on the planet—a baby, which brings out all the parental instincts—and you put the baby inside the tire. Now, is this rationally sound? No! After all, when's the last time you were speeding down the highway and a baby inside a tire passed you in the left lane? Never! But it doesn't matter. We've tested countless TV spots for GoodYear—full of rational, technical claims of superiority. And yet Michelin tires continue to sell well for something in the order of a $30 premium in America. A second example is the Reebok easy-tone tennis shoe with the extra comfortable sole. It's priced way above its rivals, and we told Reebok that was fine because when we tested consumers walking around inside of it the overwhelming emotional response was true smiles, i.e., joy. Our advice to Reebok was, therefore, don't worry about the price gap. Take the money to the bank, and be happy.

BIOGRAPHY

Francesco Ambrogetti

Francesco is Marketing and Fundraising Director for UNICEF Italy. Francesco has 20 years of fundraising experience with major nonprofit organizations including UNICEF, UNAIDS, UNHCR, MSF, WWF and the Red Cross. His experience extends worldwide and includes raising billions of dollars in Europe, Africa, Asia and Latin America. He launched the campaign "Schools for Africa" for UNICEF that raised over $200 million.

Francesco is a Professor of Fundraising at Bologna University and a frequent speaker at international fundraising congresses. He is the author of the first Italian *Handbook on Fundraising for Nonprofit Organizations* and has published several articles on fundraising in specialized blogs and magazines.

BIBLIOGRAPHY

Ahern, Tom. "*The brain according to me. Neuroscience is the most important force at work in fundraising today. Or it should be.*" http://www.txnp.org/Article/?ArticleID=14507

Ambrogetti, Francesco. *Emotionraising*. Maggioli Editore, 2013.

Ambrogetti, Francesco. "*The big chill: Can we cure donor's emotional breakdown?*" February 4, 2013. http://101fundraising.org/2013/02/the-big-chill-can-we-cure-donors-emotional-breakdown/

Ambrogetti, Francesco. "*Cry me a river: WHY and HOW emotions can save fundraising and the non- profit world,*" November 5, 2012. http://101fundraising.org/2012/11/cry-me-a-river-why-and-how-emotions-can-save-fundraising-and-the-non-profit-world/

Andreoni, James. "Impure Altruism and Donations to Public Goods: A Theory of Warm-Glow Giving." *Economic Journal*, 100 (401): 464–477. JSTOR 2234133. 1990.

Bagozzi Richard P. and Moore David J., "*Public Service Advertisements: Emotions and Empathy Guide Prosocial Behavior,*" Journal of Marketing Vol. 58, No. 1 (Jan., 1994), pp. 56-70.

Barraza, J. A., and Zak, P. J. "*Empathy toward Strangers Triggers Oxytocin Release and Subsequent Generosity.*" Annals of the New York Academy of Sciences 1167: 182–189, 2009.

Brooks, Jeff. "Show Donors the World Without their Giving." http://www.futurefund-raisingnow.com/future-fundraising/2011/01/show-donors-the-world-without-their-giving.html

Burnett, Ken. "*The Emotional Brain. Effective Fundraising, it Seems, is All in the Mind.*" http://www.sofii.org/node/1004

Calne, David. *Within Reason: Rationality and Human Behavior.* Vintage; Reprint edition, 2000.

Cialdini, Robert B. *Influence: The Psychology of Persuasion.* Harper Business; Revised edition, 2006.

Cialdini, Robert B. "*The Power of Persuasion. Putting the Science of Influence to Work in Fundraising,*" Stanford Social Innovation Review, 2004.

Craver, Roger. "*Acquisition: Premiums, Crack Cocaine And Nonprofit Suicide.*" http://www.thedonorvoice.com/non-profit-premiums-are-literally-crack-cocaine-the-why-and-how-of-stopping-the-drug-trade

Craver, Roger. *Retention Fundraising: The New Art and Science of Keeping Your Donors for Life*. Emerson & Church Publishers, 2014.

Cryder, C. E., Lerner, J. S., Gross, J. J., and Dah Ronald E., "Misery Is Not Miserly. Sad and Self-Focused Individuals Spend More," *Psychological Science*, Volume 19–Number 6 200.

Cryder, C. E., Loewenstein, G., and Scheines, R. "The donor is in the details," *Organizational Behavior and Human Decision Processes*. Elsevier, Vol. 120(1), pages 15-23, 2013.

Damasio, Antonio. *Descartes' Error: Emotion, Reason, and the Human Brain*. Putnam, 1994.

Darwin, Charles. *The Expression of the Emotions in Man and Animals*, 3rd Edition, London, Harper Collins, 1998.

Denkova, E., Botzung, A., Scheiber, C., and Manning, L. "Implicit emotion during recollection of past events: A nonverbal fMRI study," *Brain Research*, 1078143–150.150, 2006.

Dobele, A., Lindgreen, A., Beverland, M., Vanhamme, J., and van Wijk, Robert. "Why pass on viral messages? Because they connect emotionally," *Business Horizons* (2007) 50, 291–304.

Dooley, Roger. *Brainfluence, 100 Ways to Persuade and Convince Consumers with Neuromarketing*. John Wiley & Sons, 2011.

Ekman, Paul. *Emotions Revealed: Recognizing Faces and Feelings to Improve Communication and Emotional Life*. Holt Paperbacks; 2nd Edition, 2007.

Field, Pete and Pringle, Hamish. *Brand Immortality: How Brands Can Live Long and Prosper*. IPA, 2008.

Gilmore, James H., and Pine, Joseph B., *Authenticity: What consumers really want*. Harvard Business School Press, 2007,

Gladwell, Malcom. *Blink. The Power of Thinking without Thinking*. Back Bay Books, Little, Brown, 2005.

Grapsas, Jonathon. "*Is your appeal urgent?*" April 7, 2010. http://jonathongrapsas.blogspot. ch/2010/04/is-your-appeal-urgent.html

Gotschall, Jonathan. *The Storytelling Animal: How Stories Make us Human*. Houghton Mifflin Harcourt, 2012.

Guber, Peter. *Tell to Win: Connect, Persuade, and Triumph with the Hidden Power of Story*. Crown Business, 2011.

Harrison, Scott. "*Why Charity Shouldn't Be About Guilt,*" September 24, 2011. http://www.inc.com/staff-blog/scott-harrison-why-charity-shouldnt-be-about-guilt-.html

Hendrie, Doug. "*The Science of Cute,*" August 15, 2012. http://www.gizmag.com/the-science-of-cute/23707/

Heath, Chip and Dan. *Made to Stick: Why Some Ideas Survive and Others Die.* Random House, 2007.

Hill, Dan. *Emotionomics, Leveraging emotions for business success.* Revised Edition. Kogan Page, 2008.

Hill, Dan, About Face. *The secrets of emotionally effective advertising.* Kogan Page, 2010.

Hill D., and Levin A,. "*Applying facial coding to ad testing. On the face of it,*" QUIRCK's, March 2013.

Iniarra, Marcelo. "*Social trysumers and the free experience era.*" October, 13 2010. http://sofii-foundation.blogspot.ch/2010/10/social-trysumers-and-free-experience.html

James, Russel N., "Cognitive skills in the charitable giving decisions of the elderly." *Educational Gerontology,* 37(7), 559-573 III.; (2011).

James, Russel N., III, Atiles, J. H., and Robb, C. A., "Charitable Giving and Cognitive Ability." *International Journal of Nonprofit and Voluntary Sector Marketing,* 16(1), 70-83. (2011).

James, Russel N. *Inside the mind of the bequest donor: A visual presentation of the neuroscience and psychology of effective planned giving communication.* CreateSpace Independent Publishing Platform, 2013.

Landau, Greenberg, & Sullivan, "Toward Understanding the Fame Game: The Effect of Mortality Salience on the Appeal of Fame," *Self and Identity,* 9: 1–18, 2010.

Le Doux, Joseph. *The Emotional Brain (The Mysterious Underpinnings of Emotional Life).* Simon & Schuster, Touchstone 1998.

Levitin, David James. *This is Your Brain on Music: Understanding a Human Obsession.* Atlantic Books, 2008.

Lindstrom, Martin. *BRAND Sense—Building Powerful Brands through Touch, Taste, Smell, Sight & Sound.* 2010.

Manucia, Gloria K., Baumann, Donald J., Cialdini, Robert B,. "*Mood influences on helping: Direct effects or side effects?*" Journal of Personality and Social Psychology, Vol 46(2), Feb 1984, 357-364.

Merchant, A., Ford, J.B. and Rose, G. "How personal nostalgia influences giving to charity," *Journal of Business Research*, 2011, vol. 64, Issue 6, 610-616.

Merchant A., Ford J.B and Sargeant, A. (2010) "Charitable Organizations—Storytelling Influence on Donors' Emotions and Intentions." *Journal of Business Research*, 63(2010) 754-762.

Moll, J., Krueger, F., Zahn R., Pardini, M., de Oliveira-Souza, R., and Grafman, Jordan. "*Human fronto–mesolimbic networks guide decisions about charitable donation*," http://www.pnas.org/content/103/42/15623.full.pdf+html

Moscovitch, M., Rosenbaum, S., Gilboa, A., Addis, D., Westmacott, R., Grady, C., McAndrews, M., Levine, B., Black, S., Winocur, G., and Nadel, L., "Functional neuroanatomy of remote episodic, semantic and spatial memory: a unified account based on multiple trace theory" *Journal of Anatomy* 2005 Jul; 207(1): 35–66.

Olsen, Mancur. *The Logic of Collective Action: Public Goods and the Theory of Groups*, Harvard University Press, 1965. (trad. it. "Logica dell'azione collettiva, Feltrinelli, 1990;)

Pallotta, Dan. *Charity Case: How the Nonprofit Community Can Stand Up For Itself and Really Change the World*. Jossey-Bass, 2012.

Pearson, Brian. *The Loyalty Leap: Turning Customer Information into Customer Intimacy*. Portfolio; 1st edition, 2012.

Rizzolatti, G., and Sinigaglia, C., *Mirrors In The Brain: How Our Minds Share Actions and Emotions*. New York: Oxford University, 2008.

Santa Maria, Cara. "The Science Of Cute: Is Pedomorphism Why We Gush Over 'Adorable' Things?" http://www.huffingtonpost.com/2012/11/26/science-of-cute_n_2171987.html?utm_hp_ref=talk-nerdy-to-me&ncid=edlinkusaolp00000008

Sargeant, Adrian. *Fundraising Management: Analysis, Planning and Practice*, Routledge, 2004.

Sargeant, A., and Jay, E., *Building Donor Loyalty: The Fundraiser's Guide to Increasing Lifetime Value*, Jossey-Bass, 2011.

Shaw, Dan. "Use of premiums in fundraising." http://happydonors.com/?p=522

Schulman, Kevin. "Non Profit Premiums Are Literally Crack Cocaine—the Why and How of Stopping the "Drug Trade," February 6, 2013, http://www.thedonorvoice.com/non-profit-premiums-are-literally-crack-cocaine-the-why-and-how-of-stopping-the-drug-trade/

Slovic, Paul. "If I look at the mass I will never act. Psychic numbing and genocide,"

Judgment and Decision Making, Vol. 2, No. 2, April 2007, pp. 79-95.

Slovic, P., Baruch, F., and S.Lichtenstein. "Facts and Fears: Understanding Perceived Risk." In Richard C. Schwing and Walther A. Alberts, Jr. (eds.), *Societal Risk Assessment: How Safe is Safe Enough?* New York: Plenum Press, 1980.

Small, D., and Verocchi, N. "The Face of Need: Facial Emotion. Expression on Charity Advertisements," *Journal of Marketing Research*, Vol. XLVI (December 777 2009), 777–787.

Small, D. A., Loewenstein, G., and P. Slovic. "To Increase Charitable Donations, Appeal to the Heart—Not the Head" *Organizational Behavior and Human Decision Processes*. Vol. 102, Issue 2, 143–153. March 2007.

Small, D. A., Loewenstein, G., and P. Slovic. "Sympathy and callousness: The impact of deliberative thought on donations to identifiable and statistical victims." *Organizational Behavior and Human Decision Processes*, 102, 143-153, (2007).

Stephens, G.J., Silbert, L.J., and U. Hasson. "Speaker-listener neural coupling underlies successful communication." *Proc Natl Acad Sci* U S A. 2010, Aug 10;107(32):14425-30.

Thompson Walker, Karen. *"What Fear Can Teach Us."* https://www.ted.com/talks/karen_thompson_walker_what_fear_can_teach_us/transcript

Trimble, Michael. *Why Humans Like to Cry: Tragedy, Evolution, and the Brain: The Evolutionary Origins of Tragedy.* OUP Oxford, 2012.

Viard, A., Chetelat, G., Lebreton, K., Desgranges, B., and Landeau, B., et al. "Mental time travel into the past and the future in healthy aged adults: an fMRI study," *Brain and Cognition*. Elsevier, 2011, 75 (1), pp.1-9.

Wansink, B., van Ittersum, K., and Painter, James E., "How descriptive food names bias sensory perceptions in restaurants," *Food Quality and Preference*. 16 (2005) 393–400.

Warwick, Mal. *How to Write Successful Fundraising Letters.* The Jossey-Bass Nonprofit Guidebook Series, 2008.

Willingham, Bob and Matsumoto, David. "Spontaneous Facial Expressions of Emotion of Congenitally and Noncongenitally Blind Individuals," *Journal of Personality and Social Psychology*, 2009, Vol. 96, No. 1, 1–10.

Young, Chuck. "The use of negative emotions in advertising," *World Advertising Research Center*, 2006. http://www.ameritest.net/images/upload/The%20Use%20of%20Negative%20Emotions.pdf

Zak, Paul. *The Moral Molecule. The source of Love and Prosperity.* Bantam Press, 2012.

Zarrella, Dan. "New Facebook Data Proves Social CTAs Lead to More Comments, Likes & Shares," November 20, 2012. http://blog.hubspot.com/blog/tabid/6307/bid/33860/New-Facebook-Data-Proves-Social-CTAs-Lead-to-More-Comments-Likes-Shares-INFOGRAPHIC.aspx

40217688R00098

Made in the USA
Middletown, DE
06 February 2017